Best Wishes,
Dave Shors

Ribbons *of* Blue

The Life & Lore of the
"Old Pro" Pat Barnes

by Antrim "Pat" Barnes with Dave Shors

Published by the HELENA INDEPENDENT RECORD

Bruce Whittenberg, Publisher

DAVE SHORS PHOTO

To Dad
Who knew the joy of fly fishing

To Mother
Who always was ready to drop the less important things,
grab a frying pan, and cook, fresh on the stream, the fish her
family caught

To a Wife
Who thought she was marrying a school teacher, found out
he was a fisherman instead, and still stayed with the bargain
for better or for worse;
always a help
never a hindrance

To Patricia
My daughter, an English teacher, who encouraged me to put
my years of fishing memories into print.

Cover photo by Doug O'Looney
Back cover art by Kim Obata; painted after catching rainbows on the Madison on
Pat's Sofa Pillow fly.

ISBN 1-56037-119-6 softbound
ISBN 1-56037-120-X hardbound
© 1997 Helena Independent Record, P.O. Box 4249, Helena, Montana 59604
Prepared for publication by American & World Geographic Publishing

Contents

Ribbons of Blue

Foreword by Dave Shors

with appreciations by
Stan Todd and Paul Roos

The Stream, the Fly, the Fish...

As Pat Barnes was growing up in the teens of this century in Three Forks, Montana, the great rivers of the West were at his feet, Ribbons of Blue ready to be explored. As today's fisherman tries to imagine trout fishing in those days, he almost has to put himself into the fertile mind of someone like Montana artist Monte Dolack who has painted large and hungry trout swimming everywhere, in the kitchen, the bathroom, and especially in those rivers.

The Madison, Jefferson and the Gallatin, as they form the great Missouri River near Three Forks, were much the same in Pat Barnes' youth as they were when Lewis and Clark first set eyes on them a century earlier.

> (Lewis) *July 29, 1805, at our encampment on Camp Island, near the junction of the three forks of the Missouri. This morning some of the hunters turned out and returned in a few hours with four fat bucks, the venison is now very fine. We have killed no mule deer since we lay here, they are all of the longtailed red deer which appear quite as large as those of the United States....The men have been busily engaged all day in dressing skins and making them into various garments. All are leather dressers and taylors. We see a great abundance of fish in the stream, some of which we take to be trout but they will not bite at any bate we can offer them*
>
> —*Original Journals of the Lewis and Clark Expedition*
> Reuben Gold Thwaites edition, 1904

Pat's modest memories of his youth are centered on his family, which is rooted deeply in the fiber of Montana's history, and his efforts to tempt and catch the great abundance of fish in the rivers around Three Forks.

His grandfather, George W. Marshall, came to Montana in 1876 and three years later took the contract to carry mail from Virginia City to

Mammoth Hot Springs. "While carrying mail through here, I saw it would be a good location for a hotel," he wrote. The location he favored in Yellowstone National Park was at the confluence of Nez Perce Creek and the Firehole River, according to an article written by Lee H. Whittlesey in the Autumn 1980 issue of *Montana: The Magazine of Western History*.

Marshall, with the help of a partner, built the first of his two hotels in that area in 1880. Marshall did not quite have his hotel finished that fall when he and his partner used a wagon they owned to carry the first two commercial passengers into the Park.

Finished or not, Marshall's Hotel was where George and Sarah Marshall and their four children spent the winter of 1880-81, according to Whittlesey's account. The small, frontier family included Pat's mother, Lucinda. They were the first of the western settlers to spend a winter among the geysers of Yellowstone Park.

The next spring, while George was on a trip to Omaha, Pat's grandmother looked out the window and saw two marauding thieves. Grizzlies were trying to break into the storehouse behind the hotel. She grabbed a Winchester and fired. The bear she hit quit digging and charged Mrs. Marshall. She got inside and closed the door just in time, as the bear threw himself against the door. After the bear left, she followed it up the mountainside and finished the job.

When Mr. Marshall returned home, he heard about the encounter and asked: "Where's the bear hide?"

"I burned it," Mrs. Marshall said.

"You burned a good bear hide?"

Four years later, the Marshalls, with a new partner, built their second hotel near the Firehole. In 1885, George decided to retire from the hotel business; the Marshall's Hotel later became known as the Firehole Hotel.

The family then built a home on the upper Madison; the old homestead is now covered by Hebgen Lake. Later the Marshalls operated Riverside Campground on the Madison, a popular stopping-off point on the way to Yellowstone.

Pat's father, Antrim Barnes Sr., was an engineer on the Montana Railroad, the old "Jawbone," between Harlowton and Lewistown in the late 19th Century. Later, the Milwaukee Road purchased the Jawbone and extended the line into Three Forks, Butte and beyond. Antrim, Sr., then purchased a lot in Three Forks and built the family home in 1910,

One more elusive Missouri River trout meets his match.

a year after Pat was born. By that time Antrim worked three days a week as an engineer and three days as a banker in Three Forks.

Early in his life, Pat's mother taught him to fish with live grasshoppers, floating them along the swift currents of the Madison; easy pickings for the hungry trout.

"My father was a wet fly fisherman. No Montanan fished 'dry' in my growing-up years," Pat vividly remembers. "It was always a standing argument as to who was the best fisherman, Mom or Dad. Mom stuck to what she knew, grasshoppers and worms, and referred to my father's fly rod as a 'dude outfit'."

At age twelve, Pat bought his first fly outfit: a $4.95 bamboo rod, a $1 single action reel and a $15 Hardy line. By the time he enrolled at Western Montana College in Dillon, he was an expert fly fisherman who tied flies to earn extra money.

During his early school-teaching years in Wilsall and West Yellowstone, Pat worked with Montana fishing legends Don Martinez and Dan Bailey.

In 1938, Bailey opened his shop in Livingston; Montana's waters had lured him from New York and Eastern trout streams.

"He was looking for tiers," Pat remembers. "At that time I was tying only a few patterns, mostly squirrel tails, because I was teaching. I'd go down on Saturday and show him what I'd tied during the week and he'd separate the ones that looked a little different and buy the rest. Then I got the job of tying squirrel tails, because I liked them."

Eventually, as the shop grew, Bailey gave up his job back East.

One day Pat said: "Dan, you're not keeping your shop open on Sunday. Give me the key and I'll open it for you.

The first Sunday Bailey asked: "What kind of day did you have, Pat?"

"I sold a few things, a creel and some other things," Pat said.

Dan opened the till and handed Pat a $10 bill, pretty good wages in those days.

About that time, World War II changed the lives of everyone in this country.

Pat enlisted and served with the 8th Air Force in England for three years. The day he left Livingston, Dan Bailey met him at the train station to say good-bye. Bailey said there would be a job waiting for Pat when he returned home.

More importantly, Pat's wife, Sigrid, would also be waiting for his return. They were married in 1941 and Pat's dream was that he would open his own fly shop in West Yellowstone at the end of the war.

When Pat returned to Montana, the rivers were still rich in trout. In fact, they had been virtually untouched during the war years.

The summer of 1946 Pat opened his fly shop in West Yellowstone. So did four or five other soldiers who had returned to the States with similar dreams.

But Pat had an early advantage: his shop was right across Main Street from the train station. Since gasoline was in short supply, most fishermen arrived by rail. As the trains slowed in front of the depot, Pat's modest shop could easily be seen through the Pullman windows. "Pat Barnes Complete Fishing Service," his sign said.

Equipped with the best rods and reels Pat could find and the best flies Pat and "Sig" could tie, the fishermen then would walk a mile and a half to the river. Pat would wait for the next train, and another group of summer tourists would arrive to fish the Park's famous trout rivers. It wasn't long before he was guiding fishermen to the best spots.

In 1949, guiding became an official occupation when the Montana Department of Fish and Game awarded Pat its "Outfitter's License No. 2," which said he was: "hereby authorized and licensed to OUTFIT hunting and fishing parties as OUTFITTER and may for pay provide any saddle or pack animal or animals, vehicles, boats or other conveyances to any person or persons to hunt, trap, capture, take or kill any of the game animals or to catch any of the game fish of the State of Montana."

Outfitting and guiding was a new licensed occupation in the state, but it was a natural for Pat. Something he was born to do.

I was always amazed, as we worked on this book, how Pat vividly described those early fishing days, his friends and his customers.

At eighty-seven, his memories of the Madison before the "Quake," or the day Claud Aikman and a group of Texans prodded him into tying the first "Sofa Pillow," were as clear as the azure waters of the Gallatin. "Why, it's as big as a Sofa Pillow," Aikman said when he first saw the giant stone fly imitation alongside a size 16 fly.

We often sat in the den of Pat's home in Helena and shared his fishing stories. He would cant his head, close his eyes and remove us both to days that I could only imagine. The look on his face as he told his stories was one I grew to anticipate and love. The detail was always precise. The stream, the setting, the fly, the fish...they were all there, ready to be cast into the winds of our minds. Each day, "Sig" would enter our world just long enough to give us a snack of fresh rolls and fruit, and a Diet Pepsi.

I was fortunate to spend a few days on the river with Pat. His fishing skills were precise, smooth and as natural as the first morning breeze over the water.

One July day in 1996 we sat on a low streamside bench of grass along the Missouri River near Craig. Four or five fish were working the crossing currents in front of us. The Old Master honored me. He asked me for one of my flies, an elk hair caddis. He tied it on a 5X tippet and flicked it into the river. As he lifted the line off the water's surface, the power of his left-handed cast was smooth and strong. Still sitting, he laid the fly effortlessly over the river and dropped it on the nose of a feeding brown.

I walked upstream for just a minute, looking along the shoreline for my own rising fish. I looked back, and Pat had already hooked his fish. We landed it, a nice 17-inch brown, took some pictures and captured that moment on film.

It was a simple moment. But it was a special moment for two friends, worlds apart in experiences and dreams, brought together by the timeless and relentless power of the Missouri River in this land that still belongs to God.

Dave Shors

The Old Pros

by Stan Todd

Their lives followed similar, though different, paths. Pat Barnes and Dan Bailey were the "Old Pros." Unlike many of the modern-day fishing crowd, they were more interested in trout than in money. Interested in the people who fly-fished for trout, the streams that held trout, and the land through which those streams flowed.

The Old Pros loved fly fishing long before it became trendy—before it was important to be well-dressed, use the best gear, fish the best rivers throughout the world with the best fishing guides. Pat and Dan were conservationists before most people thought much about conservation.

I was the first full-time guide hired by Pat for his shop in West Yellowstone, and guided for him every summer for many years. Many of the same clients returned to fish with us year after year and, despite the fact that Pat had high standards and refused to guide people a second time if they showed no concern for conservation, his shop was busy throughout the season.

Pat introduced the McKenzie River boat to the Montana guiding community, and for a short while, he and I were the only guides using McKenzie boats. During the stone fly hatch on the lower Madison, clients would catch (and release) 20 to 40 trout, two to four pounds each, all out of what the guiding community at that time referred to as our "banana boats."

Pat and I floated the Box Canyon of the Henry's Fork of the Snake River for several years before anyone else figured out how to get a drift boat into the canyon. It was a wonderful time! Four- to six-pound rainbows were common and several ten- to twelve-pound rainbows were caught and released. Unfortunately, those days are probably gone forever.

I remember fishing with the Old Pros at Beaver Creek—a spot on the Missouri River known as a place to catch large brown trout in the fall. We fished throughout the morning with little success. After lunch, Dan caught a six-pound rainbow. Everyone was rather tickled because we had been anticipating large brown trout. As we were taking pictures of Dan and his trout, a few snowflakes started to fall. We continued fishing for another hour, but the snow started to pile up, the wind increased and the temperature began to drop. We retreated to Pat's car and decided to stick it out until the snow and wind let up. Every fifteen minutes or so, Pat or Dan would take a turn convincing each other that the storm was letting up, although it was obvious that conditions were getting steadily worse. After what seemed like hours, they concluded the storm was nearly over, but we should leave because the road was nearly impassable. Neither of the Old Pros was a young man at the time, but they weren't about to let a little weather get in the way of fishing.

Quite some time after this Missouri River adventure, I was in Dan Bailey's tackle shop in Livingston picking up some gear for Pat's shop in West Yellowstone. There was a group of fishing enthusiasts, including a fishing writer or two, and Dan. Someone asked Dan who was the best or most famous Madison River fisherman, the most notable Big Hole River fisherman, and on down the line. Dan was a very thoughtful and honest man, and he skillfully evaded answering these questions, perhaps knowing that any answer would likely be wrong or likely to offend. Finally, one person asked Dan if he could pick one person to go anywhere to catch a trout, who would that person be? Dan turned to me, winked slyly, and said, "I think we know who that would be, don't we, Stan?" And that was the end of that. I am sure Pat Barnes is the man Dan had in mind.

It is impossible for me to describe how much my life was influenced by these two men and how much their families and friends have meant to me. Certainly, many generations of trout fishermen will have a better world and better fishing because of the example set by the Old Pros.

Talented Mentors

by Paul Roos

I could write a book about Pat Barnes. For years I knew that a book had to be written. Thankfully, now it's finished. Why a book about Pat? Because only rarely do individuals (in this case we have two people, for I'm also speaking of Sig Barnes) come along who have the impact on the sport of fly fishing, environmental protection, and people as have Pat and Sig. Pat is a funny, intelligent man of extremely high integrity. And Sig has been the wind beneath his wings, his confidante, conscience, and partner. There isn't anyone I respect more than these two wonderful, talented people.

Over a span of six decades, Pat and Sig have shared their knowledge of fly fishing, their humor, and their resources with people from around the globe.

My wife, Kay, and I met Pat and Sig in the early winter of 1967. It's been thirty years. I went to work as a guide that spring in West Yellowstone for the Pat Barnes Tackle Shop. I recall the first morning I walked into the shop to go out on a training session with one of Pat's experienced guides. I wore my old fishing hat with some snelled hooks in the hat band. Without a word, Pat walked over to the counter to get some clippers, approached me and snipped off the looped leaders that were attached to the flies. He didn't even take my hat off. Right then and there I knew I had a lot to learn.

I worked for Pat as a guide for the next three years. Pat took an interest in teaching me—about fly fishing and guiding, yes. But I learned so much more about business, people, tournament casting, a healthy lifestyle, and character. Pat and Sig had a business and personal philosophy that was very simple, consistent, and successful. They just helped people, whether it was a worm fisherman or a new outfitter, a new guide or a young tackle salesman. They treated everyone with honesty, courtesy, and respect.

After the third year of guiding, Kay and I decided to start our own outfitting business back in my home town of Lincoln, Montana, on the Blackfoot River. Maybe the following anecdote tells it best.

In the dead of winter after my last year guiding for Pat, we received a copy of the newsletter Pat and Sig sent to all of their guests. It might have sat around the house for a day or two, for we were a busy family. When I finally took time to read it, I discovered an article that announced our new venture. The piece heralded us and our new location and suggested folks give us a try. That was all we needed. Our friends and mentors had given us a boost without which we may not have survived.

I have many memories—good memories, wonderful memories. But in my mind's eye I see Pat now. He's in his late 50s and fit as an athlete. He's standing in the strong current of the Madison River driving a huge Goofus Bug into the wind. He's wearing a red shirt and his old tattered wide-brim fishing hat. He's getting a hell of a long drag-free float. How does he do that?

The master guide and a former protégé, Paul Roos.

And I see Sig. She's sitting at her tying bench in the tackle shop and she's tying another Sig Barnes Ginger Goofus—the kind that I have caught 35 trout on without having the fly fall apart. As I walk in, she looks up and says, "Good morning, Paul!"

The Early Years

Will These Do?

While cleaning out an old file the other day, I found a card with six light wire #14 Alcock fly hooks attached. On the card was printed: "Horace Gardner Simpson, Architect." His address was on the card, as were the handwritten words: "Will these do?"

The card took me back some fifty years, to my first years in the tackle business. It was the summer of 1946 that Mr. Simpson first entered the shop in a dark-blue, well-tailored business suit. I remember the morning well. His was not the appearance of the usual customer, who was most often clad in wet waders, sandy shoes, a smelly fishing creel and a fly-decorated hat.

Our place of business at that time was more a shack than a shop. The floor was oiled pine boards that barely carried the weight of two roughly built log counters lining the walls. My fly-tying table extended across the back, forming a U-shaped area.

Mr. Simpson, though elderly, walked with brisk, positive, and business-like steps. In his long, slender, artistic hand he held a small black fly, a Zulu, not usually seen in our area.

My attempt to communicate with him was awkward until I realized he could neither hear nor speak. Through a series of motions, and with pencil and paper to aid us, we established an effective communications system. I was to produce his special fly on a small hook.

We were both happy and smiling when the job was finished. In those minutes a friendship developed that was to last for a number of years.

Each time he came to replace lost flies, I learned of his daily fishing experiences through pantomime, lip reading and note writing.

Those were the years shortly after World War II, when gas had been rationed and few had been able to fish Yellowstone Park waters.

The Park's Firehole River contained an undisturbed fish population.

Mr. Simpson stayed at the Old Faithful Inn and daily walked the Firehole. He was using the flies I tied for him to give the river's brown trout a bad time. He insisted on using only this small #14 fly and the very lightest of leaders.

The bears, the geysers, the tourists bothered him not at all. Since he could not hear, his attention could be focused on each bit of riffle, run, or slick as he waded through the geyser area. After catching one fish to eat each day, he then went on to catch the rest for fun.

His beat usually began at Riverside Geyser, moved up through the Upper Geyser Basin, and ended opposite the Old Faithful Inn. Along the way he stopped only occasionally to rest and enjoy the surroundings. This was his day's outing, to be repeated again the following day, and the following summer. Thus he spent his vacations, coming to town only when it was necessary to replenish his fly and leader stock.

Had you been a tourist at that time, and maybe you were, you could have witnessed his dexterity with a fly rod, the joy he seemed to have catching and keeping or catching and releasing each fish, large or small. At times he drew a crowd larger than the one watching the geyser activity. This seemed to enhance his pleasure. As he later revealed these scenes to me, my understanding would bring a smile to his aging face.

The last day I saw Horace he was on his way home. He had had another satisfying vacation. In one of our last discussions we had talked about changing hooks for his fly, the Zulu, since I had run out of the hook he preferred.

"Will these do?" he wrote on his card, and then handed it to me. Six, light wire #14 Alcock fly hooks were attached.

The hooks are still here.

Catching Chubs at the Old Slaughterhouse

In my pre-teen years, my mother seemed to love summer antics as much as I did. We would catch frogs in the swamp across the street from home, where water flooded in the spring to create a drainage that flowed out of town two or three miles into the Madison.

Hugging the south bench was another small stream of water that lazily cut through fields of cattails. It was fun to pound them together, leaving clouds of white parachute-like seeds clinging to our clothes. Red-winged blackbirds nested in the cattails and would angrily fly just out of reach as we waded through, catching frogs and toads of all sizes.

At the lower end of the swamp were blinds duck hunters used in the fall. Often the blinds were empty later in the season and we could shoot a duck or two with a .22 or a .410-gauge shotgun.

During high-water times, huge carp would cruise lazily into the slough. These too became sport for us as we chased them into the shallows where they could be caught. Then we'd sell them to railroad section workers for a dime apiece.

Occasionally, I'd follow the older boys a mile or so up the dusty road to the slaughterhouse along the Jefferson. That's where the remains of the slaughtered animals were deposited into the river, attracting dozens of fish. The choice of fish was large, but the quality was questionable. A good catch would include chubs, suckers, carp, perch, whitefish and only occasionally a rainbow or brown.

On warm summer days, fishing was interrupted when other kids came to swim. Then we'd all move up to the "Two-Bit Hole," which was deeper and had great sand beaches. We called it the "Two-Bit Hole" because swimming and diving for coins and rocks was the order of the day. Of course, swimming was done without a bathing suit.

Three or four rivers were within walking distance of Three Forks. All the kids in the gang I ran around with were fishing enthusiasts.

We fished the Madison out of Old Town for whitefish and trout, using cane poles and worms. We fished at night with sucker meat on the Missouri.

One of our favorite spots was the Cold Slough on the Madison, about four miles from town. It was a camping ground for young guys; we didn't like family there, or girls. We always caught good trout.

Early each summer, there was one trip to Wade or Cliff Lake, a campout without parents. One of our dads would drive us there and drop us off. It was a trip that usually opened the season, since most of the trout water in our area was still high and muddy. Fishing the clear water of the lakes was a real privilege.

There were years, because of late starts or flat tires, when we never quite made it to the lakes. We'd stop and camp along the Madison above Hutchen's Bridge above Ennis.

Many big fish were caught or lost. Members of our gang were brought up with the idea the best fisherman kept the most fish.

One-upmanship was an art practiced by all, both in displaying fish, and bragging about skills and techniques.

The North Bench:
A Little History

The year was 1911. Two of my three uncles, George and Walter Marshall, with financial help from my father, Antrim Barnes, Sr., had homesteaded on the North Bench, an area between Toston and Three Forks.

Railroads were advertising "free land and an opportunity to get rich" to all who would move West. Congress had passed the Homestead Act offering 160 acres of land to anyone who would live on the land for three years, while making improvements. The homesteaders dug wells, built fences and chicken coops. The Act brought an influx of homesteaders to the North Bench: Among them were the "Big Four," Mr. Townsley, Mr. McKenna, J. Jones and Ted Asher. Also, there was a "man of the town" from England—a fisherman and opportunist—Oliver Cromwell Plunkett, for whom Plunkett's Lake was named.

Those early farmers tilled virgin soil. Crops were good and other settlers came. Better buildings replaced the original homestead shacks.

It was always difficult to get help during the harvest, so everyone would lend a hand. My mother, Lucinda Barnes, would spend several days cooking for Walter, George and the threshing crew each fall.

On one occasion she needed groceries and my father, a railroad engineer, brought them by rail to Barron—a spot just a couple of miles from the ranch. There were no men to meet the train and pick up the groceries during this busy time, so it became my mother's job.

My mother had no choice but to leave her two young children at the house. I was two-and-a-half and my sister, Lucy, was four. After Mother gave Lucy instructions and admonitions covering any possible situation, she left. All went well until Lucy spotted Mother coming over the

Near Three Forks and landscape familiar to Pat Barnes since childhood.

hill on her return. Lucy wanted to run to meet her, but what could she do with a two-and-a-half-year-old brother who refused to go along? She went without me.

"Where is your brother?" were my mother's first words to Lucy.

"He's all right," Lucy answered.

"But where is he?" my Mother asked again.

"I'll show you when we get to the house."

Even in the few minutes it took to reach the ranch house, I'm sure my mother had visions of many unfortunate possibilities. But when she and Lucy stepped up on the porch, Lucy pointed with pride to a wash tub and said: "Look Mom, he's safe and happy as can be." My conscientious sister had overturned the tub, with me underneath.

This was just one of my early misadventures while I was busy exploring the world around me. Imagine my excitement one day when four big, noisy threshing machines came past Uncle Walter's house. What did I do? What any curious youngster would do—I followed them. By the time my mother checked on me, I was out of sight. Fortunately my short legs couldn't keep up with the machines, and although I was temporarily missing, I was soon corralled by Mother.

The crops were good in those early years, but they were followed by years of drought—severe drought—and no crops, not even adequate grass for the horses.

North Bench homesteaders abandoned their homes and "free land." Some moved to Three Forks or Bozeman. My uncle Walter and others got work on the railroad. Uncle George moved to the Horseshoe Hills and continued to farm for a few more years.

Oliver Cromwell Plunkett, also known as Lord Plunkett, stayed in the area. He had not been one of the North Bench wheat farmers. The land Plunkett leased had a lake on it, which was fed by a spring creek. He stocked the lake with fish and game birds. (His life in England had been one of fishing and hunting.) Then this early entrepreneur arranged fishing and hunting trips for English friends and Eastern sportsmen. Was he Montana's first fishing guide, circa 1907?

Plunkett lived in Helena when he first came to Montana, where he was a member of the Montana Club. After he moved to the North Bench he was still occasionally seen in the Capital City. A Helena paper in 1913 had an article telling how the Irish Mr. Plunkett celebrated St. Patrick's Day on one particular visit:

First he traveled up and down Main Street in an Irish buggy singing "The Wearing of the Green" and other Irish ballads. Soon he had collected a following of Irishmen and others. Then the police arrived and "informed the paraders that it was their painful duty (there being many Irishmen on the force) to announce that it was against the city charter to conduct any meeting that would block the traffic, and that, lord or no lord, the celebration of the Irish would have to cease or there would be another Irish jubilee in the city Bastille."

I met Lord Oliver Cromwell Plunkett one day on the streets of Three Forks. His reputation was widespread, and all the young fishermen were especially envious of the beautiful English salmon flies he was importing and selling in the area. He would sell those flies that were used on the streams in England to young fishermen for one dollar each; the price to others was much higher. My fishing friends and I could never afford more than one fly. We treasured them.

It became a challenge to learn to tie similar flies. Of course, I had no source for expensive feathers used on the English patterns, nor did I have the skill it takes to tie eight or more different materials on one hook. But my grandmother happened to raise a breed of turkey that had white feathers on its wings. They worked perfectly on the flies my friends and I began to tie, so I was in business at age twelve.

I have happy memories of Lord Plunkett, the North Bench, and of the big fish in Plunkett's Lake at that time.

Marshall's Hotel, built and operated in Yellowstone National Park by Pat's maternal grandparents in 1884.

Early Madison Memories

W hat I seem to remember most about hooking my first trout was how plentiful they were. Trout were rising everywhere that afternoon on the Madison. Our family was on a camping trip in Yellowstone National Park. I was six and it was 1915.

After we set up camp not far from the area that is now known as the Nine Mile Hole, my father started downstream to catch supper.

My mother prepared my equipment, a long cane pole, a bare hook tied onto a short leader and a twenty-pound test line tied to the butt of the pole and then again to the tip. To the hook she added a grasshopper. That was my "outfit."

As I glanced out over the river it seemed like I could have crossed the water on the backs of rising fish. I don't recall how many casts I made for one of my earliest catches. But I do remember hooking the rainbow, dropping my pole, running to my mother and crying out in great excitement.

By the time we ran back to the river bank, the fish and my grasshopper were gone. I don't remember much else from that day, except we did have fish for supper.

My father loved to fish the Madison, especially the water immediately below Hebgen Dam where the water pours out onto an apron and then carves a deep pool in the river bottom.

We would sit there, the whole family at times, but more often just my mother, sister and myself with cane poles and grasshoppers while my father would fly fish or cast with a Devon Minnow farther downstream.

This area from Hebgen Dam downstream to the mouth of the canyon—now Quake Lake—produced a tremendous quantity of fish. The two commercial camps, Camp Fire Inn and Halferd's Camp just above Beaver Creek, were summer homes for many fishermen. All they had to

Catch from the Madison before there was a limit.

do was step out of their cabins to catch a quota of fish. The Forest Service leased a few cabin sites and also controlled three campsites—Cabin Creek, Beaver Creek and Rock Creek. Cabin Creek Campground was on the river's edge, but has now been moved upstream; Beaver Creek was washed away by the "Quake" and is now upstream. Rock Creek, of course, is no more. It also was on the river, right under part of the natural dam.

Before I was out of the eighth grade my mother and one of her friends, Henrietta Crocket, decided to take their children through the Park. Henrietta's son, Hayden, was my age, and my sister was two years older. I don't know how they got us all in the old Studebaker.

My mother was raised both in the Park and on its borders in the 1880s and her childhood memories were vivid. She was the grand tour guide and knew every bird, animal, animal track, where the old Wylie camps had been. She told us about the history of the Park and her early experiences with animals, geysers and people.

When we arrived at Old Faithful she chose a camp spot near River-side Geyser.

"We can see it erupt from here," was her comment.

The first morning I awoke early. The camp had not stirred. I assembled my fly rod, hastened to the river and spent a glorious morning catching a breakfast of browns.

As I hurried back to camp I was followed by a smartly dressed young ranger.

Things had stirred in my absence. The young mothers had a fire going, coffee was boiling in the pot and the two women and my sister were chattering like magpies as they prepared breakfast.

The young ranger had orders to remove these "sagebrushers" immediately. But before he could hardly remove his hat he was handed a cup of coffee and was bombarded with all sorts of questions.

"Do you like cream and sugar?"

"Isn't it a lovely day?"

"The geyser display was wonderful. Did you turn it on just for us?"

When the ranger suggested our campsite wasn't really safe, my mother recalled some of her childhood experiences while camping on the very spot.

"Your uniform is so nice looking," she said. "Do you know that when as a girl I camped here, the army managed the Park? Their dress was not nearly as good looking as yours. Do have breakfast with us…"

As you might guess, the happy, cheerful women maintained their camp for three days and most of the time my mother acted as the main attraction on the geyser walks, most of which I missed.

The fish in the Firehole suffered severely.

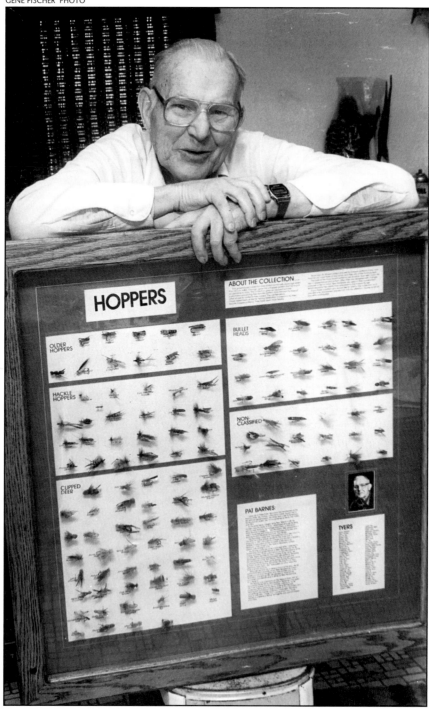

About ten dozen hopper flies are part of Pat's prized collection.

Grasshoppers:
King of the Terrestrials

As far back as I can remember, I have fished with grasshoppers, those I caught and those I tied. It was my mother's fault. She was a dyed-in-the-wool grasshopper fisher. She grew up on a ranch on the upper Madison and indoctrinated me with the concept that to catch a fish I first had to catch a grasshopper. Her other mistake, if you can call it that, was she married a confirmed and dedicated fly fisher. There was a never-ending argument in our family as to which method produced the most fish, bait or fly. My mother won out when the water was high and tinted, my father when the water cleared.

My mother's influence prevailed in my early fishing years. Her equipment, a long cane pole, a stout line, and a hopper, was a lot easier for me to handle than the outfit my father gave me, a steel telescope rod, his last year's enameled line, a dollar casting reel with a silkworm gut leader, and a fly.

At age twelve, with money from my paper route, I bought an English Halford braided line, a May Company bamboo rod, and a single action reel. The line was the expensive part of the equipment and made it possible for me to compete with my father when fly fishing. At this time, sixty or seventy years ago, few if any hopper patterns were available in stores in Montana. I suppose several of the commonly used fly patterns, the bushy ones such as the Jock Scott or the Bloody Butcher may have been mistaken by the fish for a drowned grasshopper. But if a fisherman wanted a hopper pattern, he had to tie it himself.

Thinking back over the many streams that I have fished, I can't recall a single one that hasn't produced fish for me with a grasshopper or a grasshopper pattern. Let me review a few of these experiences.

The first vivid experience I remember wasn't on a fishing trip, but on a train ride. I was about six years old and was riding the Milwaukee Road back from Chicago. On this trip, we were delayed at the town of Ringling, Montana. A slide in Sixteen Mile Canyon had temporarily blocked the tracks. While we waited, all the passengers got off the train. As Mother and I headed toward the train station, I spied on the ground a card wrapped with fish line complete with bare hooks. It didn't take Mother long to fix up a willow pole. While she was assembling the rod, she told me to catch some grasshoppers. By the time the track was cleared, she had a nice string of fish from a little creek that ran by the station.

My father was an engineer on the Milwaukee Road. Often he would come in from his run having made some previous plan with our neighbor, Ed Avery. The two families would crank up the old cars for a camping trip to Meadow (Ennis) Lake.

On one particular occasion, after camp was set up, the two fathers headed out to some spot previously rumored to produce big fish. I was greatly disappointed that I was not included in their plans. Mother, however, came to the rescue. She sent me to catch a good number of hoppers. Then we rowed to the place where Meadow Creek entered the lake and, without a net in the boat or a reel on the pole, we landed enough fish for dinner. It was a good thing that we did, too, since the fathers came back without any fish. While I remember catching these fish vividly, I also remember Ed's wife's repeated and acrimonious comments about the lack of fish caught by the two adult experts.

Fishing my mother's way with a cane pole taught me several things about one of our local meadow streams. There, the small fish were usually at the top and bottom of the pools, and the large ones were in the deep holding water. Without a reel and with one length of line, the long pole could not reach all the spots in the stream easily, but it was possible to run the bank with a large fish if necessary. Grasshoppers didn't seem to work well in the deeper spots and were not always available. Sculpins were. Tethering a sculpin off the bottom of a deep hole involved less activity, but did produce plenty of excitement if one had the patience to just sit and wait. After drifting away from my mother's method of fishing, I started using streamer type fly patterns for the large fish in the deep spots and grasshopper patterns for the smaller fish. Dry fly patterns at the heads and tails of the pools came later.

When I was teaching at Hawthorne School in Helena in 1948, my wife kept our summer shop in West Yellowstone open in September, and I sometimes commuted there on weekends. To get a little personal fishing in, I promised one of my neighbors a few fish. She said she liked small ones. Since this was grasshopper season and the stream was on my way back to Helena, with only a slight detour, I was prepared to sacrifice a few minutes of my valuable time by leaving the shop early on Sunday. Once on the stream, I quite easily took three fish as ordered from the tail of one of my favorite pools. Naturally I was using a Joe's Hopper. I whipped the fly dry on two false casts, dropped it out in the middle and started walking up toward the head of the pool. I was not prepared for the big swirl from the center of the pool when one of those sculpin lovers took my little Joe. My faith in hoppers for big fish was confirmed.

Some people do a lot of fly changing. As a general rule I choose a fly that I like and stay with it. One particular day I remember was an exception. I was fishing a #12 Royal Wulff on Odell Creek. To position myself for a better cast at the bend some thirty feet away, I moved in close to the stream bank. As I took this step, a grasshopper jumped ahead of me and landed in the water just inches from the bank. Immediately, a big brown took the hopper with a tremendous splash at my feet. I froze in my tracks. After my heart slowed up and my pulse eased, I moved back slowly. I had fished that spot with the Wulff just a few minutes earlier. I snipped the Wulff off, put on one of my favorite hopper patterns, and landed a nice bonus brown.

Then there was the time at one of my favorite spots on the Firehole River. It was well known that the best time to fish the Firehole was in the spring, before the hatches were all gone. At that time the river is clear or nearly clear and at its best temperature, and the fish, having fed all winter on their favorite insect diet, are nice and fat. The worst time to fish the Firehole, ask anyone, is mid-August; the stream is low, the water is warm, the good hatches are gone, and the wind blows every afternoon.

So let's say on August 15 you have left your rod at home. You are planning to join the sight-seeing crowd at Old Faithful and on your way home take the Fountain Flats Road up toward Goose Lake to see a buffalo. Having passed the Nez Perce picnic area, you are surprised to see a lone fisherman across the Firehole River. The poor guy doesn't know what everyone else knows, this is no time to be on the Firehole Meadows.

You slow down, wondering about this fisherman. He looks reasonably well equipped. The wind doesn't seem to be bothering his casting any. Look, the poor guy has snagged a weed bed. No. By golly, he has a fish! He lands it and then releases it. But it can't be. What does he know that "everyone else" doesn't?

Let's take a guess. The wind is blowing off that bank behind him. It must have been blowing hoppers in all afternoon. The fisherman may have hoped that trout had been under the moss bed in the shade where a cool underground spring had poured its refreshing water into his living quarters. That fish and others like him don't mind, we surmise, occasionally lifting up through warm water to pick up a nice live hopper or even a life-like one tied by Pat Barnes. That fisherman knew that he wouldn't catch many fish on this windy afternoon, but where else could he go this day to have a dry fly stream to himself, and test his skill on a wily trout under seemingly adverse conditions?

Another place he could go would be Cameron Flats south of Ennis on the Madison River. The wind blows strong down there every afternoon. It surely must blow a lot of those fat grasshoppers off the benches into the river. It won't be a place to use a small Joe's Hopper. It is larger water, so it will call for larger flies. Maybe a big Sofa Pillow, a Jug Head, or a number 6 Dave's Hopper would be his choice of patterns. The Madison River should be more productive than the Firehole. Physically easier? No, definitely not! Factors working against him as a dry fly fisherman are downstream wind, larger flies, rough and faster moving water. However, in his favor, the river should be wadeable, the water would be at a more favorable temperature, and there should be more feeding fish.

If he recognizes the need for long floats to cover as much water as possible, if he moves steadily upstream giving every fish in front of him at least one chance to look at his fly, he will come off the river thinking that this river is correctly classified as one of Montana's best blue ribbon trout streams.

I have given you two situations where grasshoppers can and have been used successfully when conditions seem unfavorable for dry fly fishing. You no doubt now may be thinking of others. I could tell you a story of nice browns taken all day long floating the Missouri in August fishing grasshoppers when nothing else seemed to work. You may have had similar experiences yourself.

With this much of an introduction to just a few of my experiences, is it any wonder that I am sold on hoppers?

I have slides of fifty hopper patterns that have been tied for and by fishermen past and present. Through research in books and articles and contact with many tiers, I have fifty names of people who have tied hoppers or mentioned them and named them. It makes a most interesting collection. Some of the tiers are professional, some amateur. Some of the patterns are very realistic, some could easily be called "Near Enough." Some you might not recognize as being grasshopper imitations, but apparently the tier thought they were and caught fish with them.

The materials used to tie hoppers vary as much as do the philosophies of tiers, but a common theme of shape, shade, and general construction runs through them all.

I have a card file listing the material needed to tie each of the fifty patterns and if something has been published concerning a pattern or the author or creator, my card file includes a reference.

As you can tell I have a streamside affection for grasshoppers and their imitations.

Thank you, Mother.

A Dream Fulfilled

The hopes and dreams of a young fisherman often take many years for fulfillment. I was born in 1909 in Lewistown, Montana. I began fishing as a young boy living in a small town near the headwaters of the Missouri River. On one of my many youthful excursions, when I was 11 years old, I found an open meadow stream where, in the fall, fat brown trout fed on small, sailboat-like insects. After many unsuccessful attempts, I gave up trying to catch these fish when they were boiling the surface.

I could, however, catch a sculpin with a screen, "lip it" on a big hook with a sturdy leader and tether it out in a deep, dark pool. There was always plenty of action before I had to go home. The fish thus caught were always "bragging fish," but no one in our town ever bragged about catching a fish on a sculpin. I followed the pattern of my elders (and the tradition of the times) and said I caught them on a Royal Coachman fly.

As I grew older and more experienced in fishing, I learned that I could take fish from this stream with a fly, and did many times. However, in the fall of the year when the water was low and the small floating insects rode it so beautifully, my skill was not up to the task at hand. I dreamed of catching just one of those fish on a tiny floating midge.

Once when I was still in my teens (and far from a purist as a fly fisherman), I was drawn into Beaty's Bug House of America in Butte, Montana, and looked over the array of flies the girls in his shop were tying. Nothing in the counters seemed to satisfy me. A kindly old gent with graying hair listened patiently to me and brought out some flies from a less conspicuous spot. They immediately struck a responsive chord. They were tiny and beautiful: segmented bodies, upright wings, a whisper of a tail, hackle tied sparse and dark. Cupped in the old man's hand

Big cast on the big river.

they rested upright on the hackle and tail with wings tilted forward as if ready to spring into flight.

In my mind's eye I saw these flies floating on my favorite pool. I could not resist buying more than I should. It meant going light on food the rest of the day. When I got home, I tucked the imitation insects away until I could try them on the gulping, slurping, surface-feeding browns. That time came.

I shudder when I recall what happened to those delicate patterns. Attached to the lightest of short gut leaders that I had in my fly box, they sank below the surface immediately. The old man who sold me the flies failed to mention that flies as well as line should be treated to help them float. Not even the smallest, hungriest or most stupid fish in the pool took a second look at my numerous presentations. They sank almost immediately, dragged under by the weight of equipment, current, or the pull of one inexperienced dry fly fisherman.

Although my first try at dry fly fishing was unsuccessful, the disappointment was not long lasting and the day was not wholly lost. The old tactics worked. When the shadows lengthened to dissolve in the dusk, the evening breeze cooled the water to slow the hatch and blow it from the water. Then the trout were willing to come to a streamer at the head of the pool.

As the years went by, I began to tie my own flies and gradually improved my skills with a fly rod. As my abilities improved, so did my tackle. In the ensuing years the tackle companies developed some wonderful high-riding floating lines and leaders that became a part of my dry fly fishing equipment.

But things happened to me. I taught school, guided and ran a tackle shop. Then I stopped teaching school and ran the shop and guided full time. I never found the time to visit that small stream with my newly developed skills.

A recent, late September Sunday gave me my chance. It was a warm day with scattered clouds moving overhead. I had a few hours free after lunch. I made a quick decision to visit the old familiar stream and pool, with the anticipation that even after all these years, things would be about the same as far as the hatch and the brown trout were concerned.

I quickly assembled my fishing gear, with a good supply of light leaders and small flies. I would attack today's problem and challenge, not as an amateur, but as a professional with a reputation at stake.

I picked up a friend who would enjoy the ride, and we were on our

Missouri River near Craig.

way. An hour or so on the blacktop brought us to a secondary gravel road. A few miles of this and we were at the turn-off gate. It seemed to have had little use. This surely must be a good omen.

We were soon in sight of the stream. I doubt that I was ever in as much of a hurry as I was now to get the rod assembled, the line through the guides, the leader attached and a turle knot tied to a dark-hackled quill-bodied midge. It was still early afternoon, and the sun had been on the water most of the day. Surely, the hatch would be on the water as well.

My friend chose to work one of the faster runs downstream with a wet fly. Glad to be alone, I walked a short distance upstream, rolled under a barbed wire fence and approached the right bank of my long neglected pool from below. Surprisingly enough, it had changed very little. Stopping well back from the water, I gazed intently for signs of floating insects and water disturbances that would reveal a feeding trout. Nothing seemed to mark the smooth flowing surface. Then I heard a slight sound but saw nothing. Had a muskrat entered or left the water?

Soon I saw the source of the sound. A fish had surfaced again just off the near bank, partly hidden by overhanging grass. Still I made no move. My eyes were adjusting better to the light. I could now see tiny upright specks on the glassy surface. I had no reason to doubt this was the same insect that I had studied on the water 46 years ago.

While I was contemplating these things, two more fish showed themselves, one on the near bank farther upstream and one on the far bank almost at the head of the pool. This was certainly different than I remembered years ago. Then, I would have had a hard time counting the fish, since there were rings within rings made by feeding fish. However, I did count myself lucky at the moment. The intermittent sound of three rising fish within easy casting distance is music to any dry fly fisherman's ears.

Several things entered into my decision to try for the fish on the far bank. From the bulge that he made as he took an insect, he looked larger. He seemed to have a regular time pattern for feeding. He was getting insects funneled to him from a narrowing feed stream between a grassy tuft and a moss bank.

This produced an excellent target. Then, too, I was afraid the leader or line might hang on the grass if I cast to either of the fish hugging the near bank. The sun was on my right and forward some 30 degrees, and while there was little danger of the fish on the far bank seeing the shadow of my rod or line as it delivered the fly, that was not true of the closer fish. Realizing this, I stepped back and planned to check the rod near the vertical on the forward cast to be absolutely sure the forward motion would not frighten the two closer fish, thus putting all three of them down.

With my eyes focused on the spot where the fly should land, I coiled out the needed loops of line, flipped the fly in the air and made a sure and positive cast to get a near perfect drop.

This fly was destined to float to where the fish would only have to open his mouth to receive it. The next moment the wheels of time ground to a stop. Although extremely small and sparsely tied, the fly seemed large compared to the natural insects in the water. The feeling of success was washed away and the old feeling of disappointment returned as my subconscious seemed to say, "It's too, too large." However, the fish was not aware of my thoughts. A bulge appeared and the fly vanished from sight as it was sucked in. Time was now racing to catch up.

I felt the tension, the first strong pull as the fish took the fly and turned down, then lighter as he reacted to the point of the hook and raced toward me from the head of the pool. Whatever an educated wrist does to secure a fly to a fish had been done. When I finished the fast stripping action and recovered the line loop, the fish was snugged taut against the bend of the rod. From there on the action was anticlimactic. The fish, after one thrilling leap, made several power runs and finally came to hand.

A young fisherman's dream had come to pass, one youthful desire had been satisfied, a reccurring dream through adulthood fulfilled. Elapsed time: forty-six years.

Guide Grant Pearson displays his catch in Pat's second West Yellowstone tackle shop.

Pat Barnes, left, and Don Martinez, center, with a customer at Martinez's shop in West Yellowstone in the late 1930s.

Pat Barnes

I grew up in Three Forks, Montana, the headwaters of the Missouri River. My mother was a Montana native whose family operated one of the first hotels in Yellowstone National Park. She taught me to fish with live grasshoppers, floating them along the swift currents of southwest Montana's famous rivers; easy pickings for the hungry trout. My father was a wet fly fisherman. No Montanan fished "dry" in my growing-up years: the 1920s and 1930s.

I remember well the fuss made over the first chubs I brought home to eat, the first trout and the first time I filled the skillet ahead of my dad, on one of our frequent family fish fries on the Madison.

My first fly outfits were my father's cast-off equipment. His tackle was typical of the local fishermen of the day. I suffered many a trip with a malfunctioning single-action reel, a well-worn line and a wobbly telescope rod. It was no wonder that when my paper route money started to pile up, I invested it in what I considered to be the best of the day. I stayed with a single-action reel and topped it off with a $15 Hardy fly line. It was the line that put me in a class with the best of the hometown fishermen.

On my own, with a copy of *Streamcraft*, I began tying flies at about age nine. Walmarth Tackle Company supplied me with what I couldn't get locally. All of the crude patterns I tied caught fish as long as they held together. My favorite patterns became the Red

Squirrel Tail Streamer, the Grey Hackle and the Royal Coachman.

In time I developed enough fly tying skills to help finance my college education at Western Montana College in Dillon. After graduation, I spent winters teaching and summers tying flies and working for Don Martinez and later, Dan Bailey.

My teaching career was interrupted by a four-year hitch in the Army Air Corps, where I served for the most part in England. In 1946, I returned to college and earned a master's degree in education at the University of Montana in Missoula. I then taught in the Helena school system until retiring in 1970.

Pat's advertising did not waste words.

My fishing hobby became a business when I opened a tackle shop and guide service in West Yellowstone. For 36 happy summers I took customers to my favorite streams while my wife, Sigrid, tied flies for them. During those years, we developed and popularized several new patterns. Probably the best known is the "Sofa Pillow," a fly that changed the traditional Madison River wet fly fishing to dry fly fishing during the giant stone fly hatch. Since then, the Sofa Pillow and variations have been used extensively on other rivers with similar stone fly hatches.

My fishing now is primarily on the Missouri River. Retirement has given me time to pursue numerous hobbies: adding to my fly collection, tying new fly patterns, making fishing nets, helping with our Missouri River Chapter [recently re-named the Pat Barnes Missouri River Chapter—Ed.] of Trout Unlimited and completing my hopper collection. I

Pat and artist Kim Obata

have seen Montana rivers at their best, and I hope that in some small way I have helped to preserve a fishing heritage for your grandchildren and mine.

The Gallatin River.

Life History of a Fisherman

• Born April 29, 1909, in Lewistown to Antrim Earl Barnes, Sr., a locomotive engineer, and Lucinda Marshall Barnes, an early Montana artist.

• Antrim, Sr. was born in Indiana and went to Purdue University. He was a school teacher, banker, locomotive engineer and a fly fisherman.

• Lucinda was born in Fallon, Nevada, was raised in the Gallatin Valley, Madison Valley and Yellowstone Park. Her father built the first hotel on the west side of the Park, Marshall's Hotel. She was a grasshopper fisher. She taught china painting and gave art lessons summers at her West Yellowstone studio and winters in Livingston.

• Age 1, moved to Three Forks, headwaters of the Missouri.

• Age 5, caught first fish, a chub on the Jefferson.

• Age 6, first trout on Ruby Creek with a hopper; first trout in the Park, on the Madison.

• Age 9, first trout on a fly, Madison, Yellowstone Park.

• Age 12, first fly outfit.

• Age 13-17, fished Madison, Gallatin, Jefferson, Little Blackfoot, Clarks Fork, Rattlesnake Creek, Willow Creek in Jefferson County and numerous small streams. Fished lakes—Cliff, Wade, Spring Creek, Hidden, Gooses, Otter, Hebgen.

• Age 18-22, fished Beaverhead, Big Hole, Bloody Dick, Yellowstone Lakes, Glacier Park's Lake McDonald, Flathead and Clark's Fork River. Tied flies to earn money for college.

• Age 22-32, tied flies during the period for Dan Bailey and guided for Don Martinez.

• Age 33-36, fished England, Scotland and Ireland while serving with the 8th Air Force.

• Age 37, in 1946, opened tackle shop in West Yellowstone; took aquatic biology course and earned Master of Arts in Education at the University of Montana.

• Age 39, began fishing the Madison River with McKenzie River boats.

• Beyond age 39, worked as outfitter and guide, tackle dealer, taught fly fishing classes in West Yellowstone, Helena, Hawaii and New Zealand.

Pat Barnes Style

My impressionistic, or "near enough" style of fly tying has resulted from a lifetime, 80 years, of fishing experiences. To explain how it developed takes me back to my hometown where the Madison, Jefferson and Gallatin rivers join to form the Missouri. These streams were my textbook.

In 1917, age eight, I tied my first fly. It consisted of a piece of red yarn and a white chicken feather on a heavy hook. It caught fish. My mother had taught me how to catch fish her way, with bait, but when I "inherited" my father's old fly rod and line, I began to fly fish.

Since I had a decidedly low income, I needed to learn more about tying flies and fly-tying material. Often on Saturdays, I would catch a ride on a Milwaukee coach to Butte (railroad families had free passes) and spend hours watching flies being tied at Bill Beaty's Bug House of America. I suppose I was a nuisance with all my questions, but I can't recall being treated other than courteously. At other times, I watched Jack Boehme and his girls tie flies in Missoula. *Streamcraft* by Holden was my textbook; fly fishing materials had to be ordered from the Herter catalog or from Wilmarth Tackle Company. Eventually, I acquired a few fly tying tools. I adapted my flies to the available materials. Crude as my flies must have been, they caught fish.

Fishing and fly tying became my hobbies throughout my school days, including college. Like others of that time and place, I primarily tied and fished with standard wet fly patterns: Grey Hackles, Black Gnats, Royal Coachmen, or various streamers.

But, after watching a fisherman catch twelve fish in quick succession on a Martinez Nymph, I became a nymph tier. The Martinez Nymph, named after an accomplished fly tier, friend, and West Yellowstone tackle dealer of the late 1930s, is still one of my favorite nymphs.

Three Forks fishermen with catch.

Upgraded to Guide

During my high school days, fishing and fly tying occupied a major portion of my time.

A group of boys, sons of railroaders, road the train to Butte on Saturdays during the winter to take music lessons. Because I was part of the gang, I went along, but I spent the day bothering Mr. Beaty who operated a fly shop called Beaty's Bug House of America.

He was a kindly old gent who answered all my questions, relevant or not. He helped me with some of my fly-tying problems. The only other fly tier in the state that I knew as a youngster was Jack Boehme, who tied flies out of Missoula. These two men were surely the gurus of their time as far as fly tying in Montana was concerned. Much of what I learned as a youth, I learned from them.

During my college days and into my first years of teaching at West Yellowstone, my fly tying provided some ready cash, plus flies for myself and my friends. The equipment was all stowed away in a small box I designed, with a hinged lid that locked to provide a base for my vise.

In West Yellowstone I met Don Martinez. He was a different breed than I had known before, a California-bred Princeton graduate, who was a hand-vise fly tier and a great dry fly fisherman. He ridiculed my flies, my use of two wets on a short leader, my cheap outfit and my waders without felt.

After I was in and out of his West Yellowstone shop for a year while I worked summers for the Forest Service, he asked me to work for him as a guide. He had upgraded my outfit considerably, as well as my skills. It was through him I became the proud owner of a 9-foot, 5-ounce Winston rod.

A Guide's Life

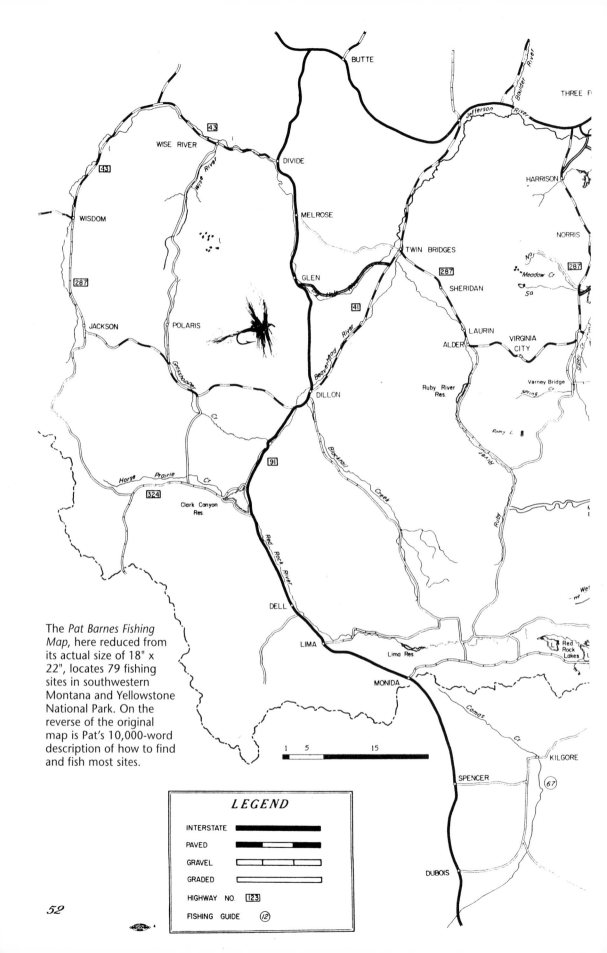

BUTTE

THREE F...

43

WISE RIVER

DIVIDE

HARRISON

Wise River

MELROSE

NORRIS

WISDOM

TWIN BRIDGES

GLEN

287

287

Meadow Cr

SHERIDAN

Sa

287

JACKSON

POLARIS

41

Beaverhead River

LAURIN

VIRGINIA

ALDER

CITY

Varney Bridge

Spring Cr

DILLON

Ruby River Res.

Romy L

Grasshopper

Cr

Fork

Ruby

91

Blacktail

Creek

Horse Prairie Cr

324

Clark Canyon Res.

Red Rock River

We...

DELL

The *Pat Barnes Fishing Map*, here reduced from its actual size of 18" x 22", locates 79 fishing sites in southwestern Montana and Yellowstone National Park. On the reverse of the original map is Pat's 10,000-word description of how to find and fish most sites.

LIMA

Red Rock Lakes

Lima Res.

MONIDA

Comas Cr

1   5   15

KILGORE

SPENCER

67

DUBOIS

LEGEND

INTERSTATE	▬▬▬▬▬
PAVED	▬▬ ▬▬
GRAVEL	▭ ▯ ▯ ▭
GRADED	▭▭▭▭
HIGHWAY NO.	123
FISHING GUIDE	12

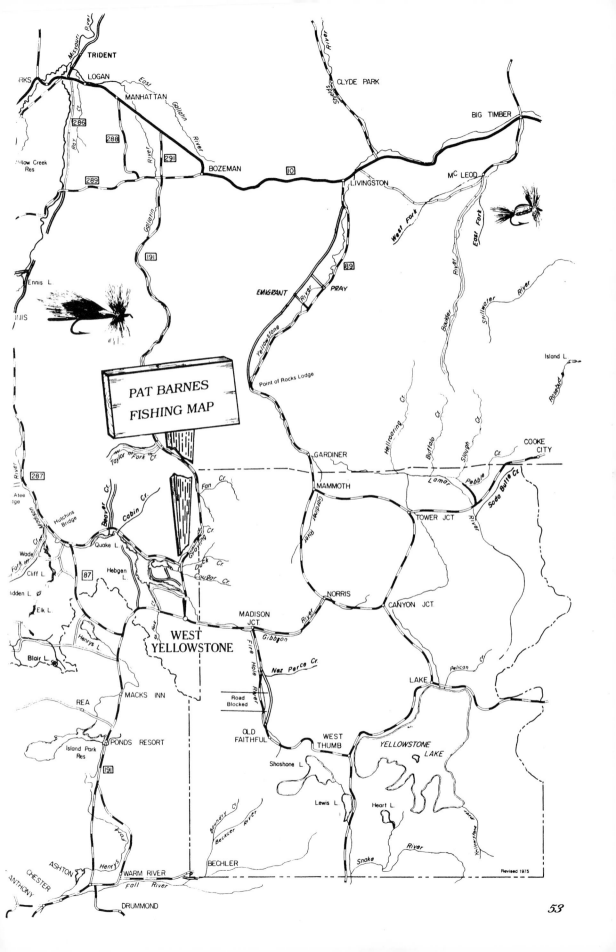

PAT BARNES
FISHING MAP

53

FEE $10.00

ORIGINAL

STATE OF MONTANA
DEPARTMENT OF FISH AND GAME

N° 2

Antrim E. Barnes
NAME OF OUTFITTER

STREET NO. OR R. F. D.

West Yellowstone, Mont.
CITY AND STATE

OUTFITTER'S
LICENSE

The above named Outfitter, whose principal place of business is in *Gallatin* County, State of Montana, having complied with the provisions of Chapter 173, Laws of 1949, is hereby authorized and licensed to OUTFIT hunting and fishing parties as OUT-FITTER and may for pay provide any saddle or pack animal or animals, vehicles, boats, or other conveyances to any person or persons to hunt, trap, capture, take or kill any of the game animals or to catch any of the game fish of the State of Montana. The above named Outfitter is NOT authorized to shoot, kill or attempt to shoot, kill or take fish or game for those employing him as an Outfitter. If the above named Outfitter is a cor-poration or partnership the herein named individual ONLY of such corporation or part-nership may act as a guide:

NAME OF INDIVIDUAL

Issued at Helena, Montana, *June 27* 19 49.

EXPIRES THE FIRST 30TH DAY OF APRIL FOLLOWING THE DATE OF ISSUE.

A. A. O'Clarie
STATE FISH AND GAME WARDEN

7   FORM NO. L-10—1M—1—1000—6-49

BY   *m. Barker*

54

Hal, Hunter and Me

World War II had ended. I was establishing myself as one of the many tackle dealers who were starting up at West Yellowstone: This had been the dream of other veterans besides myself. I may have had a slight advantage over some of them since I had guided for Don Martinez prior to my Army service and had inherited some of his customers. Among them were Hal Hentz and Hunter Perry.

It was a bright, sunny July day when they, in their black Cadillac, drove up in front of my small shop on Yellowstone Avenue. They had recently returned from a trip to Chile, where they had floated several rivers; they wanted a chance to do the same on some of the famous fly fishing rivers of Montana: the Madison, Yellowstone and Big Hole.

Because of gas rationing during the war years, there had been little pressure on our streams and fishing in most of them was probably the best it had been for years. Satisfying good fishermen like Hal and Hunter, as far as fishing was concerned, wasn't a problem. However, each was individualistic, each had preconceived notions about fishing, and each had to be educated about the fast moving waters of the Yellowstone area.

The first day we concentrated on the Madison. We were bank fishing in the area called the Hole in the Wall, just opposite the South Madison Recreation Area. Hunter and I waded to a slick behind a rock where he could easily cast to a number of spots.

"You stay here. Don't move to either side of this slick," I told him. "You can stand here comfortably, but you'll be washed downstream if you get out into the current."

"Yes, yes, I understand," Hunter said.

With the current beating against my waders, and doing my best just to stand up, I started downstream to get Hal.

Fortunately, I looked back to see if Hunter was following my instructions. What I saw was a wool fishing hat riding the surface of the water. Under it was Hunter, being washed downstream.

Luckily, I was able to catch up to him in several giant steps, and grabbed him by the arm. He was spitting water and was thoroughly soaked as I deposited him on the shore with this stern warning: "Hunter, next time you disobey me, I'm going to feed you to one of these big browns you're trying to catch."

The next day we decided to float through the Madison Canyon. (Heavy water, rough and rapid, cut through the Canyon before a side of the mountain broke off in the quake of 1959 and damned the river, creating Quake Lake.)

Hal was in the front of the boat and Hunter behind me.

As we swept down between the boulders and rapids, Hal stood up and started casting to some shoreline pockets.

"Sit down, Hal, sit down," I yelled.

But he kept on fishing. Soon I heard Hunter's command: "When Pat says sit down, you sit down."

When we finally floated out of the rough water I told Hal he could have been thrown out of the boat.

"What would you have done?" I asked him.

"I would have stuck my wooden leg up and floated to shore."

Hal did have a wooden leg. Ten years earlier an excited companion had accidentally blasted Hal's right leg while jumping up in the blind to shoot passing ducks. Hal ripped a strip of cloth from his shirt and cinched it around his leg to stop the bleeding. They finally got back to town and found a doctor. The tourniquet had saved Hal's life. But he later lost his leg.

Hal was serious. He would have floated on his wooden leg, bobbing along in the waters of the Madison until he reached shore. We all laughed as we imagined the scene.

We always laughed a lot during our trips. I never had an unhappy day with those guys. I always felt they should have been charging me.

That night, as we sat around the table recounting the day's fishing, Hal said: "Pat, in all the places we have gone, in all of the remote areas of the world, in all of the experiences we have had, we have never had the kind and quality of fishing that we have had with you."

They vowed that, no matter where they went, they would always include one trip with me each year. And they did, nearly to the last years of their lives.

Mr. Brown Takes the
Subway

Fishermen are a strange breed. As Edgar A. Guest observed, they count their thrills greatest on the fish that get away. A case in point: I ran across a fisherman friend, Howard S., on the stream. He was excited about a brown trout he had lost three days before. I listened patiently while he praised the tactics and maneuvers of this fish.

As his story went: He had been fishing the same stretch of stream with his son. He was standing on the left bank at the time, fishing upstream using his favorite dry fly, a #12 Royal Wulff, when he saw a fish rising on the right bank of a fairly long run. This particular run is unusual because it has a rather shallow and fast-dropping riffle at its head that enters a still, slow moving second channel on the far right. The current creates a deep holding pool and a long undercut far bank that offers both room and protection for such a large fish.

On one of his first casts the brown took the Wulff. The fish, he said, was well hooked. It hugged the bank as it slowly moved upstream to the head of the pool. Here it changed its tactics, coming out of the water with a husky splash. The fact that it jumped and my friend actually saw the fish was evidence enough to me that it was a fish the size Howard was describing.

This action, we both agreed, was typical behavior for a brown. Then to the surprise of my friend, and contrary to what any sane fisherman might expect of a brown, the fish worked its way up the shallow riffle, his dorsal fin out of the water much of the time. Halfway through the riffle, the fish stopped and set, an unusual move for a smart brown.

Howard gave the fish a few gentle tugs to remind it that deep water was awaiting downstream, and that if it didn't want to become trout

Pat netting a brown on the Missouri in the summer of 1996.

chowder, it better move down. Still nothing happened. Sitting there motionless wasn't sporting for either fish or fisherman.

No respectable fisherman would wade out and land such a big fish so quick and easy, said Howard. He sent his son up to the spot to spook the fish back into deep water where the battle could resume.

The boy waded out carefully, kicking a few rocks, constantly poised to jump back instantly if the bottom of the stream erupted. Still nothing happened. Then, within arm's length of the line, and in mid-stream, he reached out and gently placed his hand under the line, trying to bring the fish upward.

Still no movement.

Next he slid his hand down toward the leader only to find the fish was not there, the leader stretched parallel with the water's surface back into an unusually placed muskrat hole. The son could feel the weight of the fish as he reached back into the hole, but he couldn't find the fish.

As the son, standing ankle deep in the stream, explained the predicament, Howard realized the fish had outsmarted him. There was nothing sporting left to do but break off, reel in and give up on that fish for that day.

I was pleased to listen to this particular tale because, again, it confirmed my belief that the brown is the smartest fish in our western waters.

I assumed Howard was back on the stream trying for the brown again. He said he figured the fish must have gotten hungry, backed out of the hole and would be feeding again. He didn't think he would be fooled by the brown a second time.

He looked at me. I'm afraid my face betrayed some of my thoughts. He mistook them for disbelief and said so.

"Pat, I don't think you believe a word I told you."

I assured him I believed his every word. We exchanged a few bits of small talk before we parted. I just couldn't bring myself to tell him I had lost the same fish in the same way that very day. Nor did I tell him the next time I saw this fish feeding in the pool on the far bank, I intended to have as part of my fishing gear a gunny sack big enough to plug that muskrat hole.

Biggest Steak in West Yellowstone

As I reported for my day's assignment while working as a guide for Don Martinez, I was greeted by the news that I was to guide a man who was not the most skilled fisherman. He had already fished two days with little success.

I chose to take him to a stretch of slow moving water on Duck Creek. As we moved downstream, he caught numerous small fish. But he was used to catching big bass and these trout looked awfully small to him.

"Pat, I don't think this stream has any big fish. If you can show me one, I'll buy you the biggest steak in West Yellowstone."

He handed me the rod. Now my reputation and a steak dinner were in jeopardy.

Earlier in the day I had watched a fairly sizable fish feeding. My customer had placed his fly several times in the general area, but his casts were sloppy and inaccurate. My hope was that the fish, whose feeding had been interrupted, would be feeding again.

Luck was with me. I laid my fly in a place where the fish could easily get it. And he did.

That evening as we were enjoying the "biggest steak in West Yellowstone" my customer kept quizzing me.

"What did I fail to do? I fished the identical water. What did you know that I didn't? Was it the fly you were using?"

My answer as I remember it was: "All guides worth hiring have skills, and also a few secrets. They've learned the habits of big fish; they constantly watch the water for evidence of where fish are feeding. Guides call that reading the water. (I always wondered about that. You don't really read the water, you drink it. And sometimes you add a few drops of scotch.)

"As you continue to fish and improve your casting and other fishing skills, you will catch fish in spots where you previously failed to see any evidence of potential catches. You'll have learned one of the secrets of guides: Yes, there is an element of luck in catching big fish, but 90 percent is skill and know-how."

Riding Herd on a School of Fish

One overcast June morning, as we drove to the Madison with a carload of Texas fishermen, our car was delayed for about fifteen minutes by cattle being herded to their summer pasture. After the cattle had passed and the last cowhand had waved us on, one of the Texans remarked, "If those had been Texas cattle crossing the road, we wouldn't have moved for hours." Knowing Texan loyalty, no one argued.

The fishing car soon turned off the main highway onto a rutted lower road that led to the river. As the car approached a culvert, a gush of water from an irrigation ditch blocked its path. Again they were forced to wait.

As the water receded, trout of all sizes splashed across the road, fighting to follow the water back toward the river. When the fishermen were once again on their way, I turned to the Texan who was so proud of his state's cattle.

"How often, sir," I asked, "Are you stopped on the roads of Texas to wait for a school of trout to swim by?"

Despite the delays, fishing was good that day.

Pat was already the "Old Pro" at mid-life around West Yellowstone.

Dr. Raffle Tests the Teacher

Dr. Raffle and I had just finished a great day on the Madison. As we drove back toward West Yellowstone, he asked me a question that took me by surprise.

"Can you get a few horses for a September trip?"

"Yes, I have contacts with ranchers who have horses available. How many will we need?" I asked, still caught up in thoughts about the last rainbow of the day.

"We'll need three for the weekend of September 15."

He wanted to fish the Bechler along the Montana-Idaho border of the Park, a two-day, overnight trip. At the end of Sunday's fishing, I would be seventy-five miles from West Yellowstone. Since I was teaching in Helena and commuting weekends, I would then have a 185-mile drive back to Helena.

"How about August 15?" I suggested, but he was firm on the date.

I was hesitant, but the trip was arranged. The outfitter, horses and camping gear would be at the Bechler Ranger Station between 7 and 8 o'clock Saturday morning. Dr. Raffle, his friend Jim and I would meet them there.

It was still dark when the two picked me up in West Yellowstone. The chilly, still morning air had the feeling of fall. Grouse season was open, as was archery season for big game; a few early-morning bow hunters were pulled off on mountain dirt roads as we drove toward the Bechler.

It didn't take me long to learn one thing about the good doctor. He took the road at a more-than-average speed. (Maybe I would make my Monday-morning classes on time.)

Our plan was to camp at the Upper Bechler meadow and fish downstream. There was a good possibility a hopper fly would interest a sizable cutthroat in that stretch of water. By the time we met for lunch,

Dr. Raffle and Jim had both caught plenty of fish, but not the big one that every fisherman is looking for. We spent the afternoon fishing up toward the Falls along the beautiful timbered canyon banks. Fishing was good, but no fish in the four- to five-pound range were landed.

Sunday morning, Jim and Dr. Raffle saddled the horses. Jim went downstream, Dr. Raffle up, and I stayed in camp with our gear. There was always the chance a curious or hungry bear might dig into unattended packs.

Jim came back for lunch, but Dr. Raffle didn't appear. I kept checking my watch and thinking about my 8:30 class Monday morning. About 2 p.m., Jim and I decided to ride out in search of the doctor, and possibly a big fish. We started upstream, stopping occasionally to cast a nymph after we changed from grasshoppers.

After an hour and a half, we found Dr. Raffle's horse, but not the doctor. Even though I was nervous about the miles between me and my Monday morning class, I sat down along the stream and tried to relax by casting a nymph into the stream. The tug on my line surprised me, a strike, but he was gone. I cast upstream, not really expecting him to bump my fly again—another strike. With the third cast I had stopped thinking about Monday morning and was ready to set the hook when the fish took the nymph. Even before I landed the fish, I could tell I had a big one. Jim and I decided this five-pound cutthroat was worth keeping.

Now I turned my attention back to finding Dr. Raffle. Mounting his horse, I rode upstream, where I saw him working the river intently.

I called out to him: "If we don't head out now, I'll be out of a job on Monday."

Reluctantly, Dr. Raffle headed for camp and lunch, which was still warming on the coals of our campfire. But then he saw the five-pound cutthroat lying on the bank.

"Jim," he shouted, "where did you get that big fish?"

"In the water you'd fished, while waiting for you."

"What did you catch him on?"

"A Martinez Black Nymph."

Dr. Raffle was off his horse and into the stream before I could remind him of our need to head out, or take credit for the cutthroat.

It took another hour before he gave up the search for his own big fish. During the ride back to the Ranger Station and West Yellowstone, he continued to question Jim about the fish with visible irritation that he didn't have a five-pounder in his own creel. Jim continued to maintain the illusion that the fish was his.

It was dark before the three of us arrived at the ranger station and 3:30 a.m. when I got back to Helena, later than I had planned, but in time to meet the 30 seventh graders who presented different challenges than customers on the river.

Unfortunately, Dr. Raffle was killed in a car accident traveling to West Yellowstone the following year, and I never had a chance to tell him the real story about that big cutthroat.

The Crappies Aren't Biting

The oldtimer who had boats for rent at the dock greeted us with the news: "The crappies aren't biting; you'll be wasting your time fishing today."

However, I gave him the four bits rental fee. Somehow, I felt this was my lucky day. Margaret Voorhees, who was an enthusiastic fisherwoman, was willing to give it a try.

She selected a fly for no particular reason. We hadn't gone more than ten feet from shore when there was a disturbance in the water. Margaret had hooked a fish. It was really splashing. I didn't realize that crappies were that strong.

"We'll keep the fish for supper," I said. "Hope you can catch another one."

Since Margaret enjoyed the scenery as well as the challenge of fishing, we moved around the bend. Another fish took her fly. To our surprise it was a bass.

P.W. Nymph

Why hadn't I known there were bass in this water? Was it a well-kept secret known only to a favored few?

I asked to see Margaret's fly again and noticed it was weighted. The tail was a few strands of a duck breast feather, body was yellow with a peacock and tinsel rib. Thorax was heavy peacock shell and the back was part of a duck breast feather. Fuse wire on the bare hook or used as ribbing gave extra weight.

It had been a lucky day. Margaret had enjoyed catching the bass; I had added a new fly to my collection.

Why had Margaret's fly been a good choice? Probably because the weight carried it right down to where the fish were feeding.

This was my introduction to weighted flies where the weight was on the hook. In the "good old days," to make a fly sink I had put split shot on the leader several inches above the fly.

Margaret's fly proved to be effective in many West Yellowstone streams. She chose to name it the P.W. Nymph: "P." for "Pat" and "W." for "weighted."

The One-fish Fisherman

Mr. Windfor was one of many Texans whom I guided. He was primarily a hunter whose philosophy was a bit different than most. As he stepped into the car for our fishing trip, he said, "It's not the hunting that interests me, it's the shooting. Pat, do you understand me?"

"Yes, I think I do. You want a big fish, but you don't want to work all day finding one. Let me ask you a question. Are you an experienced fisherman?"

"Definitely, yes," Mr. Windfor answered.

"Then I think I can satisfy you," I said. "There was a time when I could take a fisherman to five spots where there was a potential of catching fish five pounds or even larger. I can't guarantee we'll see five 5-pounders, but I'll gamble that we can find a good fish. Let me give you a choice of two possibilities.

"I recently took Mr. Buck Voorhees to an area of the Madison where the wind was blowing grasshoppers into the stream. Buck was an accurate caster, followed directions well, and in spite of poor vision, hooked, landed and released a five-and-a-quarter-pound brown trout. It's about a mile-and-a-half walk to that spot.

"A second good possibility is the area known to locals as 'the cliff.' Fish live in the fast water and may be difficult to land." I knew there were big fish there since I had previously caught several.

Mr. Windfor chose "the cliff," not the mile-and-a-half hike. We drove to where my client had to cross a side channel, then cast to the other side of the river. His equipment, a 9-foot, 5-ounce Winston, would be more than adequate.

I suggested that he make his first cast to the upper left end of a log. I cautioned him to keep his backcast out of the willows.

"Excellent," I said, when after several casts a fish took his fly. He landed the fish, held up a 14-inch rainbow and asked: "Pat, is that the best you can do?"

"It's hard to predict the size of a fish in the slick," I answered. "Let's try that same area again."

Once more a small rainbow took his fly.

"Now, move several steps up river and cast your fly a foot or two above the rock," I said after he released the second fish. I knew there was deep water to the side of the rock. Many fishermen skipped that spot, expecting to find bigger fish across the stream.

"If a fish takes your fly, be prepared to follow him," I said. "Move with the fish; don't try to stop him the first few minutes."

Mr. Windfor followed my directions; his cast was accurate. A large trout took the fly as the current carried it through the deep water. Then Mr. Windfor held his rod high and kept the right tension on the fish while following it down river. The fish maneuvered toward the side channel. As the fish began to tire and move into shallow water near Mr. Windfor's feet, he handed me the rod and said: "You go ahead and land it, that's the kind of fish I wanted."

That was the end of our fishing trip.

Missouri River near Wolf Creek, early evening.

Master's Methods

Pat and his McKenzie River boat on the Missouri.

Reading the Water

Water is much better to drink than read, and better yet with a little scotch. People will try to tell you how to read water, but it doesn't really convey much. You get to know the water as you fish it. You'll catch fish where you've caught fish. Your experience on any given stream or river is invaluable.

Here are some other tips that will make you smarter about the water you fish:

1. Apply the same degree of concentration to fishing as you do to your own business.

2. Keep your fly in the water.

3. Cover the water.

4. Know your river.

5. Move fast, move slow as the water demands.

6. Try hard to get to the special spots.

7. Know the limits of your equipment.

8. Adjust to existing conditions.

9. Know your fish.

The Smorgasbord Theory

Where I grew up, we always said only a fool would fish in the middle of the day. Local custom dictated early morning and late evening were the only times to catch trout, no matter what you used or where you fished.

When I started guiding fishermen who fished for fun, they absolutely refused to believe the "early morning" bit, and they disliked late evening because it interfered with cocktails and dinner. I had to find fish for them that would take a fly during the middle of the day.

Their reasoning went something like this: It's fun to fish on a fishing trip, but it's also fun to stay up late at night playing bridge or dominoes, or to go out on the town. So don't spoil the fun of fishing by getting up too early. Let's get a good night's sleep first. Get to bed at a reasonable hour—say 1 a.m. Get up at a reasonable hour—how about 9 a.m.? Eat an unhurried breakfast, and then go and enjoy some fishing.

Of course, this isn't the approach of the dyed-in-the-wool fisherman, who is always adjusting his lifestyle to the feeding habits of the fish. The fisherman who is serious about his sport wants action. He wants to be there when fishing is best.

The expert studies the river he is fishing for the availability of the food supply. That is the prime factor in determining when the fish in the river feed. You'll find the fish where you find an abundant food supply.

I call that the "S" or "Smorgasbord" theory. Simply stated: Fish feed best, and are most easily caught, when the most food is available. That might occur during a hatch of insects, something we all recognize.

But the supply might spur feeding at unusual times. Consider these feeding puzzles which I've encountered:

• Yesterday the "gulpers" in Hebgen Lake were rising all along the

Madison Arm during the morning hours. Today, not a single fish can be seen in any of the bays and the water's surface is calm and lifeless. Then, about 8 p.m., down below Lonesomehurst, fish can be seen surfacing across the lake, up and down. They were not doing that yesterday when I drove by. How can you explain that?

• It is a hot clear, mid-July day. Clouds are building up in the west. The river is dead. We haven't caught a fish all morning. We should; the salmon flies cluster thick on the bushes along the Madison. Then a summer thundershower builds. We crawl under the boat for protection as the wind gusts and rain pounds against the boat's bottom. Soon the storm passes…and fish are rising everywhere.

• It's late summer. The water is warm, low, clear, and fishing is at its worst. It's not the time to be on the river. Then the wind picks up as you notice a farmer mowing his hay just upwind of the riffle you are hopelessly working. In minutes a few fish start to rise. You change to a hopper and start catching fish.

• You are fishing below a dam on the Madison. The water level starts dropping and goes from knee to ankle level. You tie on a streamer and in the next half hour catch three large fish, because the small fish and sculpins have been forced out of the shallows into the main channel.

• You're fishing below a railroad bridge on a favorite stream. Nothing. A freight train rolls by for ten minutes, shaking and rattling the timbers; it surely will put the fish down for a long time. Not true, the fish begin to feed on the grasshoppers and other insects that have jumped to "safety."

I contend that neither the moon nor the sun influenced the fish to feed in these circumstances. It was the "S" theory. If you as a fisherman recognize the "smorgasbord" of food available, and carry a few of the fly patterns favored by the experts in the area—the right nymph, streamer or dry fly in the correct size—you'll catch trout.

Adjusting to Wind Conditions

If wind bothers you, there are two choices: quit and go home or stay and face it. If you stay and face it, you have two choices: fight it and be miserable or adjust to it and enjoy yourself.

1. If you decide to adjust, you can do several things: change to a heavier, stiffer rod that carries a heavier line; change to a stiffer leader rather than a limp one or you may want to shorten your leader; change to a fly less subject to wind resistance. Doing any one of these things will help.

2. You might change your method of fishing. The wind direction might favor dry fly fishing over wet, or vice versa.

3. You might seek a more sheltered portion of the river, in the lee of a high bank or a bend protected by trees, a deep canyon out of the wind. I know a spot where the wind is always blowing upstream, if it's blowing, and it always favors dry fly fishing. I know a spot where an upstream wind favors my wet fly fishing. (I want to get my wet fly deep. I throw it at right angles to the stream but it is blown farther upstream. The fly then has a better chance of drifting deeper.) If you know the river, this is to your advantage.

4. You can always switch to the other side of the river if that side aids your casting.

5. Finally, you can change your method of casting. With the wind at your back use your false cast angle. Stop your rod on the forward cast 45 degrees up from the water, drop your tip, and the fly will drop to the water. With the wind in your face, turn your 90-degree angle forward. Stop the rod in front of the vertical on count one, raise your elbow high, carry the action of your forearm and rod down below the horizon-

tal. Drive the rod so far forward that it nearly splashes the water in front of you and use the second pull of the double haul. Again, shorten the length of your cast; you can get closer to fish on a windy day since the wind ripples the water's surface. Just as a rough stream bottom slows the water at the bottom of the river, an irregular ground surface slows the wind near its surface. I have had wind severely alter an overhead cast, but cause no interference on a low, side-arm cast.

If after trying these things, and any others that might occur to you on the spot, you are still in deep trouble, go back to camp or your car and wait it out. The wind will surely drop at sundown.

Time out to change flies.

Trout Can Be Characters

Trout can act much like you and I do. They can have peculiar characteristics. Let's look at a few of the "characters" I've met in our state's rivers and streams:

• **Cruiser**: Usually you'll find him in a lake, pond or slow deep pool. He is usually on the move. If he moves upstream, he'll turn and drift back with the current, feeding as he floats along. In a lake he'll work toward the shoreline, and then back out. What will he take? Usually something that looks like food coming off the bottom, like a nymph or a streamer; sometimes a tasty morsel that blew in with the wind, like a hopper.

• **Selective feeder**: Use your best imitation and present it right past his nose. He'll often take just one size of one pattern. And be careful, he's easily spooked.

• **Opportunist**: He lies and waits, watching carefully. He won't move much to feed.

• **Reluctant feeder**: He really is hungry and wants your fly, but often it will take ten or twenty casts to persuade him to take your fly.

• **Fussy**: He's only caught by fishermen who are skilled and determined. It might take twenty to forty perfectly presented casts to entice him.

• **"If it moves, take it"**: Be ready for this guy. He'll take with little hesitation, often where you least expect him.

• **Gulper**: He moves close to the surface and changes directions often, gulping spent flies in slow moving water.

• **Mr. Big**: Often he's the king of the pool. He'll move slowly and deliberately, but you'll know when he's stalking your fly. Often the commotion he causes will alarm you, causing you to lift your rod tip early; your line will come flying back toward you and Mr. Big will move back into his deep hiding place.

• **Ready but waiting**: If you place the fly in the right spot, he'll take it.

Casting:

How to Get Results

I can think of many times when one of my fly fishing friends or customers could have increased his day's catch considerably if he could have increased the length of his cast.

Most fishermen who use the short cast do so because they haven't mastered the technique of longer casts. Some have equipment that limits their distance and some don't feel the need to cast farther than they do.

Usually I can fish behind a short caster and catch as many or more fish than he, and often this results in his wanting to improve his abilities or equipment.

The short-line caster often frightens the close fish with the waving of rod and arm, and the fish quickly move out of range. If the fisherman's body motion doesn't scare the fish, picking the line off the water creates enough disturbance to warn any respectable fish of his presence. The short-cast fisherman never gets a chance to fish water beyond his casting range.

The better fishermen, who are experts in taking fish with a short cast, avoid the mistakes that send the prize darting to cover. These are the fishermen who often use the lightest of tackle, the short rod and light line. They approach feeding fish with great care, moving slowly and quietly.

But at times fishing a short line is even a disadvantage for these experts.

Often, they waste valuable time in their sneaks, when many of the fish could have been caught quite quickly and easily with a long accurate cast. A short cast also means a short float that often doesn't give a wary fish time to decide to take the fly. The short caster usually covers less ground and often ends up with a lighter creel. Does he have less fun? That I don't know.

What about the distance caster? He casts more than he fishes. Often he errs in that the sound of line speeding through the guides and the sight of it sailing across the water are thrill enough. He doesn't discriminate—he disturbs the close as well as the distant fish. The long caster often uses a long cast even when a close approach is needed.

A fishing pal who loves the long cast is often the person I would rather follow either up or downstream. He leaves plenty of fish for me.

Between Casts

You are on the Missouri, concentrating on catching the rainbow that is slurping caddis flies on the far bank. Your dry fly is in the air, then on the water...you are waiting for that strike.

What next? What do you do before the strike comes?

How about nothing? Look around and enjoy the beautiful Montana scenery.

Or you can do something. There's always plenty to do to enhance your ability to catch fish.

1. Watch your fly to see that it's floating OK. Should it be changed? Does the fly need to be "dressed"?

2. Are you stripping in some of that loose line?

3. If you're wading, what are you doing to improve your position in the river? Are you adjusting to water speed, direction, the fishermen in front or in back of you?

4. Are you more alert than you were twenty minutes ago?

5. Are you really fishing? Is your rod low or high to the water?

6. Where will you cast next?

If you are keeping most of these things in mind, YOU REALLY ARE FISHING!

Fly Casting

In fly fishing, the weight of the line carries both leader and fly through graceful loops in the air. If you're new to the sport and want to work on your technique before that critical moment on the stream when you're sneaking toward a rainbow gulping mayflies, practice a little in your own backyard.

1. Lay out twenty to thirty feet of fly line across the yard.

2. With your rod, flip the line hard and high behind you.

3. Stop the line as it begins to turn.

4. When it straightens out and starts to fall, throw your rod and forearm together with force from behind you to 1 o'clock, stopping the arm there.

5. The rod action will carry through from 1 o'clock to the water level. Your line follows the rod action and straightens out in front on you.

Fish it dry

1. Normally cast dry flies up to, or to the side of a rising fish.

2. Retrieve line in your free hand either by coiling, bunching or dropping it to your side.

3. Follow the fly with your rod tip. Why? It puts you in position to start the next cast.

4. Let the fly flow through the trout's field of vision.

5. Lift the fly off the water; the next cast is a natural 90 degree upstream movement.

6. If you're casting downstream to a rising fish, lay out a slack line and drop your rod position to water level.

Water Types

Water can run shallow to deep, deep to shallow. It moves upstream as a result of obstructions. It may be churning. There are places where the water is tailing off, increasing or decreasing in depth. You might end up fishing in any of these water types because of the sun or the shadows.

The Yellowstone River.

Knowing how these changes cause differences in the action of fish can increase the depth of the fisherman's knowledge.

I remember one day when two old fishermen were catching nothing. No action could be seen on the water, but suddenly it came alive as a summer thunderstorm passed through. In five minutes each man hooked and landed two nice brown trout, the only fish of the day.

As you develop your fishing skills, part of what you learn when you "read water" is the ability to see and develop a knowledge of where and in what types of water you find fish most often.

So even though some fishermen say they are reading the water, you'll find they actually are getting to know the water and how it changes. The better you recognize those changes, the more likely you are to catch fish.

The water may be flat and slow, it may be quick and moving. It may be moving above or below obstructions, causing deep or shallow spots. Water in streams might be tailing off, going from deep to shallow to fast moving.

To some, the changes might look like this:
- Deep to shallow, shallow to deep.
- Above, below water obstructions.
- Upstream to downstream, downstream to upstream.
- Fast to slow, slow to fast.
- From flat to riffles.
- From runs to deep.
- Increasing to decreasing in depth.
- Sun to shadow, shadow to sun.
- Clear to cloudy, cloudy to clear.
- Calm to light breeze; light breeze to calm.

In each case a fisherman recognizes the change as it takes place and it adds to his day's take.

Change = success; no change = no success.

Preventing Drag

Drag is any action that causes your line to alter the natural drift of your dry fly.

How can you prevent it from happening?

1. Hold your rod high. This keeps the slack line from pulling your fly under the surface.

2. Drop your rod to horizontal with the water level and feed the loops that develop through your line guides. This counters the force of the current.

Get Your Nymph to the Fish

Most recent articles on nymph fishing describe the deadliness and difficulty of working nymphs. Some consider this type of fishing difficult because they can't see the fly and the "take" as a dry fly fisherman can.

The weighted nymph, if used, is a little more difficult to cast and seems to need a different, stiffer rod, or at least a modification in casting technique. The nymph fisherman, to be effective, must get the fly to the fish, rather than have the fish come to the fly.

While nymph fishing is as old as fly fishing itself, it hasn't become specialized until recent years. Only in the latter years that I was in the tackle business did people come to me asking for special help with their nymph fishing.

I find people wanting to fish nymphs in their home water, which includes everything from the slow, flat, sometimes shallow spring creek, to large deep and fast moving streams similar to the headwaters of the Missouri. Lakes also attract nymph fishermen. For each lake special methods are needed.

Years ago, in small, clear, headwater streams feeding the Jefferson River in Montana, I drifted small wet fly patterns downstream on a semi-slack line and took ten- to twelve-inch trout. I felt sure these flies were being mistaken for nymphs of the many stone and mayflies. When I used instead a Sandy Mite or a Lady Mite, Pott's fly patterns popular at that time, I felt the fish were mistaking these for the many caddis larvae I kicked up from the gravel bottom. Using these same flies and a similar technique, but working upstream in the Gibbon River in Yellowstone Park in the 1930s, it wasn't too difficult to catch a limit of browns or

About to land one.

rainbows. No special system was used other than occasionally locating the trout, sometimes by sight, sometimes by judgment, and then putting the fly in the fish's general direction.

I'm sure if I were to go back to these same spots after an absence of forty to fifty-five years, I would still catch a few fish using the same flies and methods.

Were I to replace the flies with some of today's patterns, without changing technique, I would be doing a fair job of nymph fishing.

This type of nymph fishing is not the sophisticated, classical technique used today. It seems to demand a special rod, sometimes floating and sometimes sinking lines and leaders, and flies of various sizes and weight more like the nymph life in the water.

If you are an occasional nymph fisherman, stay with the equipment you have. Use it to the best advantage possible in your water by tying an assortment of flies of different sizes and weights, add weight to your leader when necessary, adjust to casting these flies with your present outfit and take with pleasure the fish that come your way.

If, on the other hand, you want to adopt the more sophisticated or classical styles of fishing used by today's specialists, you'll find you need both time and money to pursue this new adventure.

You'll need a versatile rod and several lines. Many of the lines on the market today were designed for nymph fishing. You'll find slow sinkers, medium sinkers, fast and superfast sinkers, as well as nymph tips, to name a few.

You'll need to study the nymphs in the water you fish. This is the first logical step, to find out what nymphs are present.

To do this, find a small screen and a white, shallow container. Explore the bottom of the stream in various places so you have a clue as to the kinds of life, sizes and concentrations. You might want to continue this exercise throughout the fishing season. There are a number of good books on nymph forms and a little time spent in the library will give you a general knowledge of form and characteristics. This study of insects can be carried to any extreme, if you like.

Then, in your tying or buying, simulate in form and size the most common nymphs found. I said simulate because recently while studying quite a collection of nymphs from a streambed, I tossed in a handful of my own tied artificial into the specimen pan. The thing I noticed first was both the naturals and patterns were on the dark side. When the specimen pan was gently rocked, it was not easy to tell which had hooks. Basic shapes varied no more than you'd see in people—tall and slim, short and fat. Special sizes varied from less than two millimeters to more than three centimeters.

As you study the life in your stream, you'll notice these subtle differences and you'll learn what sizes and kinds of flies you'll need.

Your choice of terminal equipment is now important in the presentation of your nymphs of choice. You'll want a nine-foot leader, at least. You'll want one floating line. Your second line will have to match your rod, but more importantly, it should be one of the sinking lines and heavy enough to reach the fish at whatever depth and sinking speed needed. The speed of the current will enter into this decision.

The rod choice stirs considerable controversy. This is partly because there are so many ways to fish nymphs; partly, too, to the fact that we are not all built the same. We all have our own likes and dislikes. Some nymph fishing demands long casts, some requires short ones; some heavy lines, some light ones. At times nymph fishing requires a sensitive tip to detect the delicate take, sometimes a stiffer tip for a faster strike and longer cast. You'll have to judge your needs.

I will say the more versatile your rod, the better it will serve you. I have found that an eight and a half-foot, two-and-seventh-eighths-ounce graphite serves me well. However, it is on the light side when casting flies heavier than 10s any distance. This is especially true if my cast is restricted.

Once you've assembled your tackle, a little knowledge of the science of reology, a branch of limnology, is very helpful. You don't really need a book for this, you can let your river be your lab.

You probably have a pretty good idea where fish lie in a stream. A little knowledge of how water moves in a streambed (reology) can help you get your fly to the fish. That, of course, is the secret of the expert nymph fisherman.

It's obvious to the dry-fly fisherman where his fly is floating, under what conditions it is dragging. It isn't so obvious to the nymph fisherman. He doesn't usually see his fly; he doesn't know where it is and whether it is floating free or dragging. He must rely on his knowledge of what his line will do in the varying speeds of current following the cast.

Just a few basic ideas to get you started in this direction:

• Water obviously speeds up as it goes from higher to lower levels; it speeds up when compressed between narrowing banks.

• Water is slowed by the banks and bottom of the stream; the rougher the bottom, the slower the water. As a consequence, the water is moving faster on top, slower on the bottom and sides. There may even be a negative current on the bottom of the stream.

A twig flowing in the main current may be moving five miles per hour, the average flow is three miles per hour, and at the bottom and sides, less than one mile per hour.

You may have seen an insect crawling along the bottom of a stream where you would think the speed of the current would wash it away. Because of the "coarse sandpaper effect" of the bottom on the water, the insect is in zero current.

Your observations as you watch your line, your fly, sand and pebbles you kick up as you wade, sediment along banks, these all give you clues to help you get your fly to the fish.

If you are fishing a variety of water, finding a variety of conditions as most streams offer, it isn't a bad idea to keep mental notes on how you caught each fish: on the bottom, on the top, in the current, on the edge, at the top of a pool, at the tail, on a dead drift, following a retrieve, the kind of retrieve.

As in all new water you fish, cover it all. It is great fun catching a fish where you least expect one. Good luck with your nymph fishing.

The Slack-line Cast

The fly fisherman who lays out a perfect loop and a straight line fits beautifully on a striking Montana postcard scene. There surely are places and situations where that kind of cast is going to produce fish, and lots of them.

However, most of the time I fish dry flies on moving water, so most of the time I am casting upstream to the right or the left of the rising fish. If I use the straight-line cast, the drag of the line sets in too quickly—then the fly skirts across the water and is pulled under and another cast is needed. It's exactly what I don't want my fly to do.

The remedy is the not-so-beautiful cast—the slack-line cast, the lazy "S" cast, or whatever you want to call it.

How do you make the slack-line cast? Remember when you first learned to fish and you could easily lay out forty feet of line over twenty feet. Go out and see if you can still do that. If your technique is as pure as a hatching mayfly and you can't, hand your least favorite outfit to a beginner and let him show you the technique. Watch him carefully. That's the lazy "S."

There are other ways to get the same effect. You can put extra force into your cast—use the effort to cast fifty feet of line when you only have forty feet stripped off your reel. Or you can just abruptly stop the shooting line when the fly is over your target. One of the easiest ways to lay down a nice slack line is to "cast up the hill," cast toward the top of the trees, the canyon, the clouds, whatever is conveniently located about 45 degrees overhead. When the line straightens and starts to fall back into the water, drop your rod with it.

Any of these techniques will probably give you a nice slack line, a lovely float and a fish. The casual observer who watches you land the fish and release it will wonder about you: "How could anyone with such a sloppy cast catch such a nice fish?"

Nymphs and Floating Line

One March day, Keith Draper and I drove about an hour northwest out of Taupa, New Zealand, to explore a stream that Keith had fished many years before. We had heard reports on the fisherman's grape-vine that a large brown had been caught there and we wanted to verify the existence of others.

While the trip provided little in the way of big fish, it did allow me to see Keith work a pool with a nymph in a beautiful setting. As I stood in the tall grasses along the bank, Keith demonstrated both his skill with a fly rod and his ability to properly fish a wet nymph up-stream on a floating line. It was deadly for the fish, and productive for the fisherman.

Keith's technique for fishing a nymph upstream differs in several re-spects from the traditional dry fly methods.

The nymph fisherman must know the water, where the fish are most likely feeding. Then he must have the skill to control his fly and direct it to those spots. The fly must be weighted so it will sink to the proper depth, where it will bounce or drift with the current along the bottom, free of drag.

The drift of a dry fly along the surface is seen; what happens to your nymph as it drifts toward you is conjecture. Experience tells the fisher-man whether his fly is being mouthed by a fish, is bouncing off the bottom, or has hit a snag. Keith's advice to his pupils is: "If there's any pressure at all telegraphed to the tip of the rod from the line, a lift should be made instantly."

Let's assume we are with Keith. He approaches the ideal nymph pool from downstream where the water is smooth and flat. As he looks to-ward the head of the pool, there is some narrowing of the water; the flow is now faster to the left bank, slower to the right. As his eyes move downstream, he sees that the depth gradually increases from his right to his left.

As he studies the stream, it's obvious to him the deepest water will be just below the riffle at the top of the pool and along the left bank, hence the most likely spot for the best fish.

Nevertheless, he lays a straight line out to the middle of the pool, covering the lower half. As the line drifts toward him, his tip is down, the line is gathered in concentric loops. He lifts it out of the water with a roll cast; two false casts remove the loops from his left hand and the fly, leader and line are laid out straight again, just two feet to the left of his first cast. He gradually works his way toward the bank.

The most popular method of fishing wet is to cast across and float down. Use a slack-line cast to get a longer drift; cast high, pull back and cast slack. You can use sinking or floating line to adjust the fly to the food level. If you feel the nymph or streamer isn't deep enough, you add weight to either the leader or the fly. You can also cast a little more upstream.

The action is the same, whether you are fishing with a nymph or streamer. The fly is inching along the bottom, flowing free with the current. Your rod is low to prevent drag. When the fly has moved through the pool, you lift the rod and prepare for the next cast as the line and fly surface.

If you are a nymph fisherman fishing with a weighted fly, you might modify the action just described. Hold your rod high, parallel to the water, keep less line in the water, and follow the bouncing fly as it moves along the bottom.

Quick Lesson in Fly Fishing

1. Have the best reel, line, rod, terminal tackle you can afford.
2. Be alert, observe the water, wind, insects, banks; in short, watch everything around you.
3. Study the water for currents and movement.
4. Fish the best-looking spots first. Spend more time on them, but cover all the water.
5. Move fast through water that is usually unproductive; move slowly through your best spots.
6. Keep your fly in or on the water as much as possible. Eliminate needless false casts.
7. Avoid drag.
8. Cast above and allow the fly to float well through the pocket.
9. Follow your floating fly without distraction.
10. While your fly and line are floating, hold the rod tip parallel to the water.
11. Keep line below the first guide under your reel hand.
12. When stripping loose line, strip behind your rod hand.
13. When playing a fish, keep rod at a 45-degree angle.
14. Give line when a fish runs; take in line when fish slows.
15. Land a fish as quickly as possible.
16. Keep a fish in the water as it is released by removing the fly. If you plan to keep the fish, it should be spent and lying on its side before you try to land it.

Fishing the Midge

When fish are hard to catch on traditional wet flies, dry flies or streamers, the use of floating fly line with a fluorescent, highly visible tip makes it possible to catch those that are nymphing, that is, fish that are tailing, exposing their dorsal fins and tails to the surface.

For years, people who have found this situation, i.e., visible tailing fish, have come to me in frustration, asking for advice. They try everything, but find it impossible to catch the fish.

Often, the best advice I could give them was to "sit tight, wait them out," go back to the spot when conditions are more favorable and try again. This answer never really suited anyone.

Recently, while experimenting with a floating-tip line, I came up with an idea. I found it worked in a variety of situations: when fish were tailing in smooth, flat, slow-moving water; in still ponds; and in streams where tailing fish were not visible.

This method may not be as exciting as watching a floating fly dance down a riffle. It may not produce the thrill you feel as a trout "takes" on the turn with a wet fly, but the method does produce fish when others fail.

I'm sure you have heard of midge pupa nymphs. You see their discarded cases floating on the surface after the insects fly away.

The idea in this type of fishing is to imitate the live insect, produce a fly that resembles the midge and tie it with enough weight to get it under the surface. Your leader must be adjusted for the fly to sink without hanging up on the bottom. Cast the fly quartering upstream. *Watch the line tip as carefully as you would a dry fly.* Allow it to drift through the feeding fish (if you are in moving water), inch it in if you are pond fishing, and for goodness sake, strike softly when the tip of the line *dips.*

It sounds simple enough, and it does work. Important things for you to remember:

• Study the type of midge nymph in the water. Tie yours life size or larger. I have found Midge Nymphs will take fish even though they are two or three times oversized. With the help of some friends, we have worked out a few patterns that work well in our area. Perhaps they will work equally well for you. We have tied our flies on hooks as small as 18 or as large as 12.

• Use a reasonably long leader, at least ten feet, especially if you are fishing in clear, slow-moving water. Know the depth of the water you are fishing. A stiff leader works better than a soft one—fewer missed strikes. Use line dressing on your leader next to your line if there is any chance the fly may settle on the bottom, but be careful to keep it off that portion of your leader near the fly. Your best bet is to dress only a short portion of your leader and only dress more if your fly is dragging on the bottom.

As I said earlier, you will cast your fly quartering upstream so it drifts into the feeding fish. Allow it to drift through the area. Then carefully inch the fly back for the next cast, so you don't disturb the feeding fish. Once a fish is caught, it may take several minutes before tailing fish are seen again.

In faster-moving water, more fish will often be found near the tail of the pool. My experience, however, is that the better fish will be taken up front. Obviously, you will know the strength of your tippet and will adjust it to the size for the largest fish in the water.

This method has worked for me and I know it will work for you.

Fishing the Weighted Spider

The method just described for fishing the midge nymph can also be used with other fly patterns: standard wets, the soft hackles, and other nymphs, both weighted and unweighted. Some slight modification is needed in each case.

However, the secret is to give the fish an artificial close in appearance to its food. Then, you have to put it within reach with little or no water disturbance, but with action typical of the food being presented.

I have experimented with some success in situations where tailing fish have been hard to take using a weighted "dry fly." Sounds like a paradox, a weighted dry fly? You must be kidding!

One thinks of a dry fly as being one tied on a light wire hook with enough stiff hackle to hold it above the surface film. The same fly pulled under the water would be a sunken dry fly and normally would be picked out of the water immediately.

I can remember one time when a fisherman showed me a fly used to take a nice mess of fish. I looked at the fly, and since the hackle was at right angles to the hook, I asked the innocent question, "Did you fish this fly dry?"

His answer brought surprise, doubt, even wonder to my face. "Nah, I fished it wet."

He had fished a dry fly as a wet fly. He probably didn't know the difference.

But it got me to thinking. "Why not intentionally build a weighted fly with stiff hackle at right angles to the shank of the hook and see what results I could get."

Several attempts didn't work. But then I came up with one that did. It was a weighted Spider Fly, with the essential difference being it was tied on a foreshortened shank, it had a fat body and of course, it was weighted. The hackle was oversized, like all spider flies, but it was tied Palmer.

It's fished much the same as the Midge Pupa, i.e., cast upstream with slack in the line of drift. Watch the tip of your floating line constantly for the telltale dip. If you're fishing a lake or pond, retrieve it slowly; let it drift normally if the water is moving.

DOUG O'LOONEY PHOTO

Pat's left-handed cast is easily recognized on Montana rivers.

Pat's Principles

1. Never tell where you are going to fish, only where you went yesterday.
2. Fishermen are all a little crazy. The only way to tell how crazy is to listen to their fish stories.
3. When you cast to a rising fish, it is more important how you cast than what you cast.
4. Fishing is a sport one can enjoy for a lifetime.
5. All the stories about fish that have never been fooled, or fishermen who have never failed, are false.
6. Versatility in fishing is the key to continued success.
7. Don't fool around changing flies. Get to know the water and patterns that work. Pick one, then keep your fly on the water, that's where you catch trout.
8. You catch fish where you caught fish before; what you learned ten years ago still applies today.
9. Scratch a fly fisherman and you might find a worm fisherman.
10. Fishing is better than playing the horses or heavy drinking.
11. The hardest thing for a fisherman to master is patience.
12. Fishing is a sport where the greatest enjoyment comes from using the lightest equipment.
13. To a rising fish, your first cast must be your best cast.
14. Sure ways to lose a fish are to give him all the time in the world or to try to horse him in.
15. Fish spend 90 percent of their time on or near the bottom, 10 percent or less near the top and no more than a half of one percent in between. But the big question for the fisherman is: Where is the fish now?
16. Doing what is hardest to do is one of the things that makes dry fly fishing the most fun.
17. The hero in our story is the fish, whether he gets away or is kept. The villain is you, if you keep him.

Why Did I Miss That Strike?

The question our guides hear most often: "Why did I miss that strike?" It's a simple question, with hundreds of possible answers; Look at the factors that lead up to the moment of connection between fly, fish and fisherman, then you'll understand.

Weather, water, fish, and fisherman all play an important part.

The important thing, if you miss a fish, is to succeed in the next attempt, when a whole different set of circumstances may come into play. That makes the guide's job difficult, because he has to be alert; he has to analyze the exact situation and convey the facts to the fisherman who wants to catch the next fish.

Let's imagine you just missed a nice rainbow and you ask your guide that common question. What's his answer? Be patient, it might take him a while to consider all the possibilities.

First, let's have your guide look at variations in water conditions. A strike on fast water is different from one on slow water. A surface strike involves a different set of reactions than a submerged fly strike. A taut line strike is different from a strike when the line is slack. The speed of the current and the location of the fly in relation to the current might influence the timing of the strike.

Let's take a situation common to many mountain streams. The current is moving two to four miles per hour, water volume is 500 to 1,500 second feet, water depth is varying anywhere from two to six feet, and the fly is floating. The fish sees the fly and is determined to get it. He's in his own backyard. He shouldn't have any problems, should he?

Let's examine the water he lives in. The water is gaining speed at various levels up from the bottom, where less resistance is encountered.

It is slowed by obstructions just under the water, and by rocks sticking out of the water. The flow accelerates with increasing gradient, and slows on flat spots. There are often forces moving the water and the fly laterally, irrespective of what the fisherman does or does not do. A rock divides the water unevenly because of its shape; more water moves to one side or the other. Or, a sudden breeze over the water shifts the fly's position.

All these complexities might be easier to understand if you imagine your hand is the head of a fish. Submerge your fist under a fly on the water and see what happens to the fly as your closed hand moves toward it. Predict the direction the fly will move down the slope made in the water by your hand. It's hard to do, and even harder for the fish trying to take your fly. Sometimes it's amazing the fish is able to get the fly at all.

While it is hard to anticipate or enumerate all of the water factors that might keep a fish and a fly from ever connecting, I think it's important that you recognize these many factors do exist and that most of them are beyond your control.

Realizing this, you can have more fun fishing and you won't blame yourself for every missed strike.

But water conditions aren't the only variables.

What about the fish? Can we isolate him from his environment? Let's try.

Just because a fish moves toward a fly doesn't mean he intends to take it. If you have fished for long you've seen fish follow a fly, possibly a streamer; you've seen fish play at taking a dry fly and actually nose it out of the water; and you've seen fish make a pass at a fly, turn short, turn back and actually take it. Often, in situations like these, you're trigger happy and take the fly away too quickly.

Many a rainbow has cleared the water to take a fly on his way down. Even when the skilled dry fly fisherman is alert to this type of attack and leaves his fly on the water, the fish often misjudges the position of the fly and misses.

Or the fish takes the fly, opens its mouth to force it deeper and the fly pulls free. No, he didn't spit it out. Look at the mouth structure of a fish. Is the tongue long enough, the lips and jaws mobile enough to spit out a fly fast? Hardly. About all he can do is open his mouth, turn his head and leave the fly to the side.

Once in a while the fish seems to move so close to your fly that it seems like a strike. But the fish refuses the fly at the last instant for any one of a number of reasons. Drag may have caused the fly to speed up so the fly drifted beyond his feeding area. He may have refused to follow it out of a protective pocket, or he may have seen a larger fish and turned away.

A light from a shiny rod, a bank vibration, a seagull winging overhead are a few of the other unpredictable things that make a fish change his mind at the last moment.

Fish, at times, also have peculiar actions. A brown trout occasionally lines up downstream from a fly, drifts down with it as he examines it critically, then slows up and lets the fly move to him. If this happens, the tendency is to strike too fast. You see the fish. The excitement builds. You can't stand seeing that fish so close to the fly without going into action. No action, of course, is what you want. Hold off until you see that mouth close on the fly, and then the strike. A gentle up-lifting on the rod will do the trick. Don't strike too hard.

"Why did I miss that strike?"

Well, we blamed the water. And, we had to blame the fish. What about the fisherman?

Of course, it could have been the fisherman's fault. The reaction time might have been too fast or too slow.

Reaction time is that period between the times when you know what to do and you actually do it. It's your fault that you missed the strike if you are either too fast or too slow in your reaction. It's really not too hard to decide what the fisherman is doing wrong and how to correct it.

Here are a few rules to guide you if you decide you are too fast:

1. Concentrate on a smaller circle of vision around your fly. If you are still too fast, look away from the fly, concentrate only on the feel of the rod and wait for any increased pressure on your rod tip.

2. If you are wearing Polaroid glasses, take them off.

3. Raise your rod tip slightly.

4. Try relaxing a little.

5. Squint at the fly, watch only the surface, do not attempt to focus on depth.

If you are striking too slow, do the opposite:

1. Concentrate on a larger area around the fly.

2. Put on your Polaroids.

3. Lower your rod tip to near water level.

4. Anticipate the direction of the fly's drift and concentrate on that area.

5. Concentrate on movement below the surface.

A lot of negative things can happen. It's amazing we ever catch a fish. But as often as not, it all comes together. The water carries the fly perfectly into the trout's feeding area. He times his rise; the fly is in his mouth (after all, he's worked his entire life to perfect this action); your reaction is impeccable. The fish is on!

Leaders

Some fishermen complain they can't get their leader to "turn over." What should they do?

a. Straighten the leader by pulling it along the back of a shoe or a piece of rubber.

b. Match the diameter of the leader butt and the fly line, as closely as possible.

c. Add more force to the cast both fore and aft.

d. Make sure leader knots easily slide through rod guides.

e. Adjust the end of the leader to the size of the fly.

f. Increase tippet size for larger flies. A Sofa Pillow is hard to turn over with a 5X tippet.

Should a leader be clear, opaque or translucent? It should be clear so it doesn't cast a shadow on the bottom of a smooth flowing clear stream.

Should a leader float? No.

Landing Large Fish

You've practiced all the mechanics of casting. You know where to put your fly, so you cast it and the fish takes. You have only one problem left—getting the fish into the creel.

The principles of landing fish are simple, but the execution of the principles isn't always as easy. During the excitement of the jump (if he makes one), the swirl he makes when he takes the fly, the singing of the reel while he runs, the continual pounding he gives the rod as he turns in the current, these are the things that cause adrenaline to flow and cause our hands to turn to stone on the reel. Often the fisherman just stands there in awe, doing nothing, or doing all the wrong things.

One old-timer who had caught hundreds, maybe thousands, of fish in his life once said to me. "I have just discovered a new way to lose a fish; I got my fingers tangled up in the line when he ran."

He certainly knew better, but he also recognized there are lots of ways for a fish to get away. Enumerating them now won't help you much. You should have the pleasure, or displeasure, of discovering them streamside, yourself. What you do want to know are a few basic principles to think about and practice so nothing will keep you from landing the big wall-fish when he comes along.

Do's and Don'ts

1. Maintain the handle of your rod near 45 degrees off the water. Never raise your rod behind the vertical.

2. Give line freely on the initial (fast) run, don't give line he doesn't earn.

3. Stay as close to the fish as the conditions warrant, don't let him take out too much line.

4. If a fish gets downstream, don't expect to bring him back; follow

him down with lateral pressure and keep below him if possible.

5. Don't be in too big a hurry to follow a big fish upstream. Chances are you will be retracing your steps later.

6. Don't try to reel in slack when he runs toward you. It's too slow. Strip line in by laying the line under the fingers of the rod hand; strip below the rod hand.

7. Get the fish in as fast as possible without undue stress, but don't gamble on forcing him into shallow water before he is tiring.

8. Keep rod pointed in the opposite direction the fish wants to go; never pull a freshly hooked fish against both weight and current unless that's the only alternative.

9. Dip your tip to a jumping fish, but put him back on tension as he drops back into the water.

10. Don't try to net a big fish with a small net, it's better to find a spot to beach him.

11. Have enough backing on your reel to handle a run of the largest fish in the river.

12. I'd like to advise you to maintain a constant tension on the fish, but I know it can't be done and shouldn't in some cases: when he shakes his head; on the jump; when he runs toward you. This applies as well to the expression, "Keep a tight line." Any attempt to keep a tight line at these times is apt to end your relationship with the fish. Playing a fish requires give and take. You give when he goes, you take when he slows.

13. Don't listen to the guy on the bank telling you what to do. By the time he yells, "Give him line, give him line," chances are he should have been shouting, "Strip, strip."

New Ways to Lose Fish

A person might think that after seventy years of fishing, one would have mastered all the techniques of losing fish. However, I guess it is not so. While fishing the Missouri one day, I worked from daylight to 9 a.m. before getting a strike. It turned out to be a nice fat and deep male rainbow that I decided to keep. I landed him without incident and cleaned him carefully, since this was the first rainbow of the season. As I looked at him, my mouth watered as I anticipated how nice he would taste filleted and fried in a skillet.

I made the mistake of working back out into the higher-than-usual river and concentrating too much on catching another just as nice. Some fifteen minutes later I climbed back out on the bank, went to the spot where I had carefully laid the fish on a thatch of grass. Not a sign of the fish could be detected. I walked the strip between bank and river three times, checking the places where I had landed and cleaned the fish.

The fish just was not there. I rationalized that even cleaned he might have flopped once or twice and wiggled into the water. However, grass along the bank would have hindered him from floating away.

I lost a fish once to a mink and thought maybe it had happened again, but a mink would have left tracks on the still-soft sandy bank.

I gave up finally and in a short time was lucky enough to catch another fish. This time, when I placed him on the bank, I marked the spot well. I laid him on some grass in full view and only waded out a short distance from the shore.

I became conscious of all the usual river sounds—crying of inland gulls, chirping of blue birds and scolding of magpies. I could hear water murmuring around the rocks and riffles as I watched an immature bald eagle soaring above the canyon walls. It seemed the eagle had one eye on my fish, so I thought he might have been the culprit.

Interspersed with the familiar sounds, I found myself picking up the conversation of two crows. At first they were high on the tree-covered canyon slope. I watched as one hopped and dove down the staircase of trees toward my fish. His mate sat back some thirty yards on a dead limb making diversionary sounds, ready to give a warning if needed.

When the lead crow dropped to the ground near my fish, I knew it was time for action. I cried out a war whoop and headed for the bank in a splashing, waving action. Two crows simultaneously sounded the retreat. I tied the fish to my belt, secure in the knowledge the mystery had been solved and I had just discovered another way to lose a fish.

No trout, especially the first trout of the season, should be carried away in the bellies of two very black crows.

Fish can be lost in plenty of other ways. Here are a few I have discovered.

How to lose a fish

1. Grabbing the line when the fish is running downstream.
2. Getting loose line tangled in the reel handle, fingers, feet or things underfoot.
3. Getting the line fowled in the line guides.
4. Allowing too much slack when the fish has not been securely hooked.
5. Failing to check for and take out any backlashes or knots in the line.
6. Allowing the tip of the rod to drop too low to the water.
7. Setting the reel's drag too lose or too tight.
8. Allowing the fish to run too freely or too far.
9. Failing to follow a fish on his run downstream.

Mistakes made by experts

1. Experts often cast too long, too short, too straight. Be alert on all casts, even the back cast.
2. Tip UP! You were told that by experts. It applies when a fish is on, not before the strike.
3. Improper strike: Good fishermen don't strike a fish, they set the hook. You hear them talking about the "strike of all time." Only rarely does a fish strike a fly. He usually takes it if the fisherman will let him.
4. Experts tend to adjust fishing hours to their convenience rather

than adjust to the feeding habits of the fish they want to catch.

5. Experts often leave a fly on the water longer than necessary or they pick it up before a fish can react.

6. They fail to do what they know how to do. An example: Coil line properly.

7. They reel to excess, or make too many false casts, wasting time.

8. Experts take their failures too seriously.

9. They assume the stream knowledge they have applies to all water. While fish are the same, food and stream conditions are not.

10. Experts rely too much on one fly pattern.

11. They don't pay enough attention to accuracy.

12. Even the experts believe you can't catch a fish until you put your feet in the water. Many think you can't catch a fish until the water is at the very top of your waders.

Thrills of Fishing

Where do you find the greatest thrill (pleasure) in fishing?
1. In the beauty of the places it takes you.
2. In the skills you develop.
3. In the strike.
4. In the action during the play—the jumps and runs.
5. In developing a fly similar to the trout's food.
6. In the association of fishing friends.
7. In the pursuit.
8. In the final release.
9. In the reflection of past experiences.
10. In the raw association with the elements—wind, water, rain, the fish itself.
11. In displaying the fish caught.
12. In taking your son or daughter, or any boy or girl, and sharing their excitement.
Some people think that on one end of the line is, yes, a fish. On the other end is a sucker. We won't call those people fools. We'll just enjoy what we share.

Flies Tied
and True

The Fly-tying Machine

by Sigrid Barnes

On a sunny August afternoon, a tourist from California sat in our shop. (We had two chairs reserved for "tired" fishermen or for the "armchair" kind.) He had been watching me tie woolly worms. "Mrs. Barnes," he said, "You ought to have the machine our son builds. You'd be able to tie two flies in the time you now spend on one."

Sig and the machine.

That sounded interesting. I always seemed to have more fly orders than I managed to find time to tie. We ordered the machine.

The machine was built on a sewing machine base—the 1920 treadle kind. The treadle had been split. Instead of the tier making the winds on the fly, the tier guided the materials while the vise rotated. The split treadle allowed for rotating either backward or forward, and allowed instantaneous stops.

The original machine had one weakness: It took two hands to tighten the hook in place, leaving neither hand free to position the hook in the jaws of the vice. A new head and a simplified tightening mechanism were designed and built by a friend, Walter Gwaltnig, who worked for Caird Engineering and was once a student of mine in Wilsall.

The machine became a tourist attraction. Fishermen who tied their own flies would take out a watch with a second hand and time the tying of a woolly worm or other patterns. Teen-age boys would say to their dads: "If you'll buy me that machine, I'll tie your flies for you."

The machine was retired in 1981, but can be seen at Boy Jacklin's Tackle Shop in West Yellowstone. My standard answer to the inevitable question: "How many flies have been tied on the machine?" was, TOO MANY!

Thrill of Tying Flies

For the person who wants to get the ultimate thrill out of fly fishing, I suggest you tie your own flies. For a minimum cost of equipment and materials, good flies can be produced that will catch fish. Many items you'll need can be purchased in your fishing area. Possibly some items might have to be ordered from firms that deal exclusively in materials for fly tiers. Other materials, such as feathers and fur, can be obtained from friends who are hunters.

Most people like to do things they can learn easily. Without too much trouble, most of us can produce a fly that will catch fish. Yet a hobby must be challenging in order to hold our continued interest. Fly tying is certainly that. There are many types of fly patterns to imitate and there are a great number of techniques to master. When you have learned them all, you can work to speed up each of your tying steps, or you can even experiment with new patterns or techniques. Fly tying helps you extend your sport to the after-fishing hours and the off season. When you venture forth with your new creations, real adventure is yours with each cast and each time you change to a new pattern.

The height of achievement for a fly tier comes to the person who a selectively feeding fish (one that is feeding on a particular insect and no other) and who goes to his kit and produces a fly that will imitate the natural insect and catch the fish.

Someone once said that much of the fun of fishing is in the wishing. Your wishes will come true oftener if you tie on your own flies. There is always the possibility that you will make a better fly than any that have been made to date.

The Sofa Pillow

Right after World War II, Claud Aikman asked his Texas friends to join him in a trout fishing trip to West Yellowstone.

They arrived ahead of Claud, driving their Cadillac loaded down with Texas bass fishing equipment. That's where the trouble began. Claud wanted them to have a good time, so we sent them down to the North Fork of the Snake. They stumbled through the water, lost their glasses, reels and flies. They didn't know they had to grease lines and flies. To make a long story short, they didn't have the faintest idea about where to cast or how to fish for trout.

Sofa Pillow

So they all came back to our tackle shop. I told the Texans what to do and said I'd go with them the next day. We gave them the material and fishing equipment they needed. They fared a little better, but couldn't float a small size, sparsely hackled fly. That required practice and patience.

Claud came to town and we gave him a report about his friends.

"If they're going to catch fish," he said, "they're going to have to fish dry flies. But what kind of a fly can you produce that these men can float? If these fellows have good fishing, they'll come back year after year."

I started experimenting with a long-shanked size 8 hook. I gave the fly a wing of red squirrel, and a heavy collar of brown saddle hackle. This would give good floatability, plus it would cast a shadow about the size of a large stone fly (commonly called the salmon fly) that was on the streams at the time.

The next day, I put one in Claud's hand next to a size 16 fly.

"My gosh! That's as big as a *sofa pillow*!" he said as he sized up the pattern.

"You named it," I said.

Thus the Aikman Sofa Pillow was born. His Texas friends caught big fish, and lots of fish, the rest of that trip.

That's about when Keith Canyon and Bud Marvin of Salem, Oregon, came in and asked, "What are those Texans fishing with?"

We gave Keith and Bud a few Sofa Pillows and they took the flies, and me, to the Madison. The natural adult stone flies were everywhere, fluttering around the bushes and trees and falling spent on the water, so Bud and Keith took my advice and got ready to fish our monstrous imitation in the Box Canyon.

They stepped down off the bank into a spot in the Box that locals called Garbage Can Number Two and immediately started catching fish. Two Idaho fishermen were standing nearby drifting eggs down through the long runs with no luck. One of them called over to Bud, "What you using?"

The two-pound rainbow Bud had on kept him busy for a minute or two. Then Bud shouted back, "A Sofa Pillow."

About this time Keith hooked a big rainbow that headed across river, behind a rock and into some fast water, and the second Idaho fisherman yelled, "What did he take?"

Keith immediately shouted back, "A Sofa Pillow!"

All was quiet for about five counts. Then the first Idaho fisherman crawled out of the water up onto the bank and shouted to Bud and Keith, "You guys, go to hell!"

By the way, the Texans returned to fish the North Fork of the Snake and the Madison River during the salmon fly hatch many, many times. During the 1966 season the same old gang fished the Sofa Pillow for the first time on the Yellowstone River and were in the hatch for nearly a week.

The popularity of the fly increased each year. It was fished during the grasshopper season, and successfully. Soon it was being tied commercially by all tiers in the West Yellowstone area.

It is now tied as large as size 2. The original fly had a red tag, red wool body, red fox squirrel wing and brown saddle hackle. Many variations are now used, in body color, body material, wing material and color of hackle. The changes Sig and I have added to the fly in recent years are the addition of a Palmer brown hackle on the body and elk hair under the squirrel hair.

It is doubtful if any dry fly in recent times has been used as successfully for catching big fish in rough water.

Pat's Favorite Flies

I'd hate to be the person to say these are the flies you should use. I'd like to say, "I've found these flies have served my purpose."

If you opened my fly box, these are the patterns you would probably find, flies used by myself and our customers between 1920 and 1990:

• Four common nymphs: Black Nymph, Pheasant Tail, Pat's Weighted (P.W.), and Harriman.

• Assorted sized Adams; probably the most popular dry fly used on Western waters.

• Five early winged wet flies, still popular on small streams today: Western Bee, Royal Coachman, Black Gnat, Wickhan's Fancy, and Cow Dung.

• Eight assorted small dry flies: Blue Dun, Hendrickson Quill, Grey Goofus, Ginger Goofus, Caddis, Renegade, Elk Hair Caddis and Grass-hopper.

• Larger size dries: Royal Wulffs, House and Lots, Ginger Goofus, Renegade.

• Ten mixed wets and dries. All have had or are now being used with great success: Silver Doctor, Scud, Mickey Finn, Spruce Fly, Hopper, Bloody Butcher, Muddler Minnow, Sofa Pillow, Jug Head, and Pat's Improved Sofa Pillow.

• Red Squirrel Tail (the Trude), which is always effective on the Madison. It's a fly I picked up when I was twelve years old and I've never been without two or three in my tackle box. It's one I tied for Dan Bailey for a year and a half before the war.

Every fisherman has special flies. For me, the Red Squirrel Tail has caught as many memories as fish.

One warm summer evening after my last year in high school, I was on Ray Creek, casting to fish rising to mayflies. I was fishing at the tail-end of a pool and the fish were piling up. All of a sudden I looked up and there was a man behind me, a wealthy rancher dressed in a business suit.

"Son, you know you're fishing my water," he said.

"Yes," I said.

He grabbed my line and pulled it in. "You don't mind if I look at that fly, do you?"

He studied the Red Squirrel Tail.

"That's a Trude," he said. "What's your name, son?"

"Antrim Barnes," I replied.

"What do you want to do with your life?" he asked.

"Go to college," I said.

He asked me other questions. Then, as he started to leave, he said, "I'm glad to see you. Let me know when you get ready to go to college, I may be able to help you." That never came to pass, although he did help several other young people from Three Forks with their college expenses.

His name was B.S. Adams. In Three Forks all the lots were set up by B.S. Adams. My father built our home on one of those lots.

I continued to fish his stream for many years.

You had to cross a barbed wire fence to get to that stretch of water where we had talked that summer night. On the corner fence post there always was a steel sign: "B.S. Adams Properties."

The years passed. Whenever I saw the sign it reminded me of B.S. Adams and how our conversation that day made me feel good about myself. Gradually, a few rust spots worked through the sign's white paint. Then one day I noticed the sign had fallen off the post into the high grass.

I took it home.

Flies We Made Popular

These are a few of the flies we made popular during the time we had our shop at West Yellowstone. Some are patterns we created, others we thought we improved, some were common patterns that suited our customers and fishing conditions of the area.

Sofa Pillow. We created this fly the year after the war to imitate a floating salmon fly. Claud Aikman had a group of Texas bass fishermen in West Yellowstone on a fishing trip. They couldn't catch fish with what they had. Claud asked me to tie a fly that they could see, that would float and would catch fish. I tied the first one, Claud named it.

Super Sofa. Sig tied this one. Other dry fly patterns were being tied with the claim they would float better than the Sofa Pillow. This fly, on which a Palmer hackle and elk hair under the squirrel hair were added, was our answer.

Jug Head. A similar fly was tied by Betty Hoyte, one of our customers. She wasn't a professional tier. Betty didn't have enough dry-fly quality hackle to tie the Sofa Pillow, so she added a flattened, clipped antelope hair head in place of the heavy collar of brown hackle. We recognized its good floating quality and added it to our stock of salmon fly patterns. One of our guides, probably Lloyd Bray, named it the Jug Head.

P.W. Nymph. Buck Voorhees kept bugging me for a weighted nymph. Buck was a retired college professor, one of our steadies. I was looking for something that would satisfy him, something that I could tie fast with the materials at hand. This was one of the several he liked. It became a hot seller when a camera man from St. Louis caught a five-pound brown on the P.W. Nymph on the Firehole. He enlarged the picture of the fish with this fly in its mouth showing plainly. He gave a copy of the picture to both Bud Lilly and myself so we could hang it in our shops. I enjoyed having Bud display "Pat's Weighted Nymph," the P.W. Nymph, in his shop.

Pat's Hopper. It would seem that everyone who ever tied a fly tied a version of the grasshopper. This was one of ours.

Martinez Nymph. I worked for Don Martinez one summer before the war. This was the nymph he sold. The same winter I tied flies for Dan Bailey. Dan didn't have a similar nymph in his shop. This one worked well in the spring

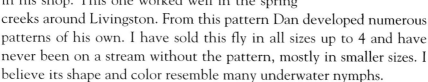

Pat's Hopper

creeks around Livingston. From this pattern Dan developed numerous patterns of his own. I have sold this fly in all sizes up to 4 and have never been on a stream without the pattern, mostly in smaller sizes. I believe its shape and color resemble many underwater nymphs.

Goofus Bug. The original fly came from California with Jack Horner. Jack was a talker. He claimed it caught fish everywhere. The fly he showed me was tied with one bunch of deer hair and one gray hackle. I was not impressed. He said he could tie one in a minute. I was still not impressed.

But later in the summer on Cliff Lake, with rising fish and a California customer, I cast one of Jack's specials, tied to a 6X tippet. I struck a fish, lost the fly; tied on another from his box. One cast more in a different direction, another strike, another fish. This one came to net with my first fly in his mouth, leader dangling. I was impressed. I removed both flies, put the fish back, put the first fly in my hat with the leader dangling.

When I told this story to fishermen the next day they asked for a similar fly, goofy as it was. We kept busy tying this fly the rest of the summer under the name Goofus Bug.

House and Lot, also **H&L** or **Hair Winged Variant**. President "Ike" Eisenhower fished Colorado. This was his favorite fly. He called it the House and Lot because he felt that if you owned your house and lot you didn't need anything else, except this fly. An issue of *Collier's* magazine told the whole story.

H.L. Variant

Dan Bailey and I read the story in *Collier's* and, from the description, tied Ike's fly. Our flies turned out different. Mine is the one now carried in Dan's catalogue. It is a great fish catcher. When Herb Wellington from New York state and his many fisherman friends fished the Ennis area they found the Eisenhower fly one of the best. We do not use the Ike name in print;

it's patented. I've always wondered how close my pattern comes to the one Ike used.

Hopkins Variant. The Hopkins Variant was introduced into the West Yellowstone area by Donald S. Hopkins and he used it in the many areas he fished. Don was a friend as well as a customer, and always a conservationist. He also was a perfectionist in all of his sporting activities. We tied this fly for Don and his friends during the many years we were in business.

Green Drake. Green Drake patterns have been around for a long time. Colonel Frierson, first a customer, then a guide, then a friend who liked to go along on guide trips and move my car, filled a wonderful spot in my heart. He often told me tales of his fishing experiences. The military took him throughout the world, and whenever he could he fished for trout.

He never kept a fish and frowned at me when I occasionally let a customer keep one. He was the first person who told me about mayfly fishing in New Zealand. This Green Drake was his pattern and it produced great catches long before other patterns were popular.

Nymphs from Pat's Fly Box

If you want to become a nymph fisherman, or if you are an old hand at it, we have four nymphs you should have in your fly box. They are tied to imitate the stone fly nymph (Plecoptera), the dragon fly and damselfly nymph (Hemiptera and Odanta), and the mayfly nymph (Ephemeroptera).

Nymph patterns other than these four are tied to imitate the smaller crustaceans often called fresh water shrimp, a few of the two-winged insects (mosquito larvae, for example), a few of the beetle family that are water inhabitants, and possibly the caddis worms (Trichoptera) imitated best in this area of the West by the ever popular Pott fly patterns.

At one time we used just one fly to imitate all underwater insects, the Black Nymph. When Don Martinez introduced this fly into our area in 1937, he exploded the myth that nymphs had to be flat. The Black Nymph is not weighted, it is tied on a regular shank hook in all sizes ranging from 6 to 16. Of course, as its name states, it is black. It has a natural mallard breast tail, copper ribbed black fur dubbed body, thorax of black chenille backed with green raffia, and finally one turn of grizzly hackle for legs.

I complained to Don once about the sparseness of the hackle. In his own sharp and critical way he said emphatically that this simple wrap of hackle was what made the fly so effective. I feel now that the Black Nymph is taken by fish because it resembles a stone fly.

Dragonfly nymphs generally tend to be shorter than the stone fly, their abdomens larger, with segmented bodies much less tapered. To imitate this nymph, we started tying the P.W. Nymph in 1954, a fly inspired by one of our customers, Buck Voorhees.

Since then, the P.W. Nymph has taken a lot of fish. It is weighted, tied on a regular shanked hook with body shape similar to the more common dragon fly nymphs. The colors in the fly are green and yellow. It too has mallard breast in its construction, its tail and dorsal thorax covering. The body is yellow yarn ribbed with lead wire and peacock herl. The hackle is sparse and is part of the thorax covering turned back toward the eye. This makes it a rather quick pattern to tie.

For the damselfly nymphs we use a Needle Nymph that was first brought into our area by two men known to us at the time only as Smith and Jones. They hailed from the West Coast, arrived in August when the fishing was tough, and insisted each day when they came in from fishing that we display their catch. Since they kept our display box filled with five-pound fish, and they seemed to be doing it so easily, we just had to have a copy of the fly they were using.

They called their fly the Pink Petuti and they claimed they were catching fish in Lost Lake.

Just like their names, which were not Smith and Jones, they were not catching the fish in Lost Lake and the Pink Petuti was not pink. It was a fly hackled with the soft green feather from the Chinese pheasant over a slim, long green yarn body. When they ran out of their own flies, we tied them others with various colored bodies, and they were just as effective. We learned an unusual fishing technique, too, that was part of their secret. They fished with a waterlogged line, using a slow, hesitating retrieve.

Smith once confided that he and Jones were really "at convention." I never did learn who was standing in for them.

The Pink Petuti's popularity grew after the two characters had to return to work. I still use it today.

"Near-Enough" Theory

Fishing and fly tying were my hobbies throughout my school days, including my college years. Like others of that time and place, I primarily tied and fished with standard wet fly patterns: Grey Hackles, Black Gnats, Royal Coachmen, or with various streamers.

But, after watching a fisherman catch twelve fish in quick succession on a Martinez Nymph in Duck Creek, I became a nymph tier. The Martinez Nymph, named after an accomplished fly tier and West Yellowstone tackle dealer of the 1930s, is yet today one of my favorite nymphs.

As a fly tier for Dan Bailey's Fly Shop in Livingston the summer of 1939, I gained a wider knowledge of patterns and improved my technique; my flies were being sold commercially. After dreaming about owning and operating a tackle shop for forty-five months while in the 8th Air Force in World War II, my dream materialized in May of 1946 when I opened a shop and guide service in West Yellowstone.

Because of what I had learned under Dan Bailey's expert tutelage, and because of the availability of better materials and seven years of practice, my flies were becoming standardized. Did they catch more fish? I never could prove that to myself. Hence, my "near-enough" theory.

Just a few of my many experiences and observations that further confirm my belief:

1. Perrault's Dictionary of Fishing Flies.

Would you believe that a book of fly patterns by Perrault contains a listing of 16,000 flies? I met the author a few years ago in Ennis. He expressed the opinion that there probably were thousands of additional patterns that could have been included. Certainly this suggests that trout are opportunists and will generally take whatever comes their way.

2. My first crude fly.

For you fly tiers who spend ten to twenty minutes producing a perfect imitation of a stone fly, can you explain why my first crude fly, tied when I was eight years old, took fish? And what about the first fly you tied? I would believe it caught fish, although it might have been a poor replica of any choice morsel of trout food.

3. One hundred thirty hopper tiers can't be wrong.

Recently, when I asked a large number of fly tiers to each send me a favorite grasshopper pattern, 130 responded. The contrast in patterns was amazing: There were flies with the usual turkey wing, plastic wings, hair wings, or no wings; rubber legs, peacock legs, straw legs, or no legs; bodies were yellow, red, green, palmered, fat or thin. This collection further confirms my thinking: fish are not programmed to only one realistic grasshopper pattern.

4. Even my wife wouldn't believe this one.

One day while fishing the fast waters in the Madison Canyon below Hebgen Lake, I landed a three-and-a-half-pound brown. What I had caught it on is immaterial to this story; what the fish had taken previously was a rock, one and a half inches round. I am not suggesting that you load your already heavily weighted fishing vest with stones of this size, nor do I have any suggestions as to how you would fish the stone if you did, but it is obvious to me that this fish didn't stop to investigate whether the stone had six legs, or eight legs, or no legs at all.

5. A trout is a trout the world over.

During the 80 years that I have fished Montana streams and lakes, I have stuck pretty close to a few choice patterns. The water has varied from small brooks to almost unwadeable rivers. I have used these same patterns in England, Ireland, and Scotland where fly fishing has been a sport for generations; in Australia, Tasmania, and New Zealand where fly fishing is relatively new; and in Alaska and Canada. My favorite flies have been productive in all these places.

At one time, Dan Bailey's Fly Shop had a customer whose businesses took him all over the world. Wherever there were trout, he fished. Was his fly box filled with innumerable patterns? No, he used various sizes of one pattern only.

6. Spying on a pair of browns.

Over the years, I have enjoyed watching trout behavior in streams. One October day, while duck hunting along the Shields River north of Livingston, I noticed the tail of a run, two browns in fairly shallow water. The one above was nosing over rocks, stirring up the bottom; the trout below was feeding on whatever material looked inviting to him as it drifted by. After a while, the two changed places. The interesting part of this operation was that each trout in turn sampled a wide variety of materials, choosing some, rejecting others.

Excited by this observation, I exchanged my gun for my fly rod. My strategy would involve catching the lower fish first. The problem now was what should I use. These two fish were definitely feeding underwater. It was somewhat illogical to use a dry fly, but in order to avoid disturbing the upper fish, I selected a high floating Grey Wulff. The four-and-a-half- and five-pound browns that took my dry fly compensated for my duckless day.

In this particular situation, as well as others that I have observed, I have found a common feeding practice of trout: alone or together, they take from the river whatever it provides. The need for an exact pattern of fly doesn't seem to exist in these situations.

7. The brown and the wobbler.

After an absence of four years from the teaching profession due to World War II, I felt a need for some refresher courses, so I enrolled at the University of Montana at Missoula. Along with the not-too-exciting education courses, I signed up for an aquatic biology class taught by Professor Bronson. On a field trip, the purpose of which was to analyze the contents of the stomachs of fish in the Blackfoot River, only one student (me) succeeded in landing a fish. It was a seven-inch brown caught on a five-inch lure. Why this trout refused to take a stone fly imitation and instead was attracted to a lure is beyond my comprehension. With an abundance of food available in the stream, we could only speculate as to why the fish took the lure.

8. Those happy and "crazy" Henry's Lake fishermen.

The fishing in Henry's Lake in Idaho attracts about the same group of fishermen year after year. There is a continual competition among these fishermen as to the size of fish caught and the number. Certain areas in the lake are especially productive. The fisherman on Monday who finds this area is the kingpin for the day; his fly pattern is the "hot" pattern. On Tuesday there's a new area, a new fly pattern, and a new kingpin. The number of different "hot" patterns my wife tied for Henry's Lake fishermen while we were in the tackle business in West Yellowstone certainly exceeded the varieties of insects in the water. And at times, these imitations failed to even remotely resemble any living thing. Yet each of these innumerable patterns took fish when fished in a special "secret" way in the right spot.

9. On changing flies.

When I first started fishing the Missouri River where Beaver Creek enters, I saw only an occasional fisherman. Big streamers and big fish were the order of the day. What I often did was put on a Muddler Minnow, catch my first fish, switch to a Mickey Finn, catch a second one, change to a Spruce Fly or even a Woolly Worm, and continue to catch fish. If fishing was good, any of these and other patterns worked. If fishing was poor, none of the flies took fish. From this, I have concluded that fly patterns are only one of many factors that determine a day's catch.

The Goofus Bug

In the ever-changing world of fishing, flies come and go. There is one pattern that is here to stay. For fifty years the Goofus Bug has been a standard bearer. While primarily a western dry fly, the pattern's versatility and its ability to adapt to new materials have literally made it popular around the world.

It's been a pleasure taking part in the evolution of the Goofus. Its history is rich, and it's entertaining and somewhat insightful to follow the Goofus on its journey through time.

The original version of the fly was tied in the early 1940s by Jack Horner of San Francisco. It was, by today's standards, akin to the Model T. Simple and basic, named the "Little Jack Horner," it was tied with a hunk of deer hair for body and tail, using black winding silk. Generally, it was tied on hook sizes 10, 12 and 14, with deer hair ends not split into wings as they are today. The fly was introduced to the West Yellowstone area by a customer of Jack's.

The Goofus

On a placid and stunningly beautiful day in July of 1947, a visiting angler hired me to guide him on now-famous Cliff Lake, where several Montana state record rainbows have been caught. The experience that day was pivotal in launching the fly's journey to popularity.

It began really as a debate about the virtues of rods. Knowing I was a Winston rod fancier, he cajoled me into making a few casts with his new E.C. Powell rod. Clearly, it was the only way to resolve the debate. On the first cast, a trout rose to the fly, but promptly disappeared as I set the hook and snapped the leader.

"What size tippet?" I asked.

"Gut 5X," came the reply.

I spend several minutes tying on a new tippet while we drifted unanchored in a light breeze.

"What was the fly?" I asked.

"Little Jack Horner," he answered.

Borrowing another "Little Jack Horner," I made a cast with the Powell rod. This cast, too, produced a rise and a take. This fish was boated only to find the lost tippet and the first "Little Jack Horner" embedded in the trout's jaw. I unhooked both flies, released the fish, handed the rod back and placed the first "lost fly" in my hat, complete with tippet.

The next day, behind the counter at our fly shop in West Yellowstone, several fishermen noticed the leader dangling from my hat. The story of the two casts ensued. At the end of the story, the invariable result was a request for some of those goofy-looking flies. My wife, Sig, complied by tying them on the spot.

The following year Montana guide and fly tier Keith Kenyon adapted the "Little Jack Horner" through the use of elk hair and blue dun hackle. He called it his "secret weapon for the Firehole River." An aura develops around any fly that is allegedly secret, and soon the requests for that "goofy deer hair fly you tie" began to escalate. The name "Goofus Bug" was adopted. I would venture a conservative guess that during the next forty years, my wife and I tied and sold more than 40,000 Goofus Bugs through our West Yellowstone fly shop. Many generations of Montana, Idaho, and Wyoming trout have risen to this productive pattern.

In the early 1950s, Dan Bailey became a believer in the Goofus Bug while fishing with me on the Snake River. Upon learning of the fly's simple materials and easy construction, Dan coined the name "Poor Man's Wulff." The following year the Poor Man's Wulff showed up in Dan's catalog in sizes 10, 12 and 14, tied with red, green, or yellow floss underbodies, distinctly divided wings and deer or elk hair upper body and tail. The 1989 Dan Bailey catalog featured four distinctive patterns of Goofus Bugs, clearly a testament to the fly's productivity and perseverance.

In 1972, an Orvis representative asked if I knew of any new or unique dry fly patterns. I showed him the Goofus Bug. The 1973 Orvis catalog premiered a new fly called the "Humpy."

It was Jack Dennis, Wyoming author, fly tier and tackle dealer, who really popularized the name Humpy. He blended the Goofus and Royal Wulff, using calf tail for wings, a red underbody, and moose hair for the tail, to create what he called the "Royal Humpy." In 1974, the fly became the focal point of the cover of his book, *Western Trout Fly Tying Manual.*

In the 1970s, a fisherman friend introduced the fly to England by taking the prize fish in a private river, to the astonishment of the natives. He kept the fish. This led to the banishment of both the fisherman and the Goofus Bug along that private stretch of river.

The Goofus Bug arrived in New Zealand in one of my fly boxes in the early 1970s. It was popularized there by guide and tackle dealer Robert Speden of Te Anau. It is now a well accepted dry pattern for the rivers down under.

Jack Horner's original idea back in the 1940s was a good one. While the fly has undergone an evolution of adaptations and materials, the basic concept of design is what makes the fly productive with trout, and, as a result, popular with anglers. No doubt, its evolution will continue, to the entertainment of fly tiers and enjoyment of fly fishers for generations to come.

Marked-down Flies

In nature, most animals line up in what is commonly recognized as a pecking order. One animal in the group dominates, others fall in line. At the end of the line there are one or two subservient to all the rest. Those are in real trouble and probably won't survive to reproduce.

Fish are much the same. I am sure there is one fish in every pool or stretch of stream that occupies the best position for food and shelter and dominates the living area.

In this same pool or stretch of water, any fish that behaves abnormally, swims differently or exposes itself to danger is immediately attacked, soon to become food for other fish.

The idea of attracting and catching fish with lures that behave in odd ways is popular with many lure fishermen. I remember being on an aquatic biology field trip back in the 1940s. I was assigned to catch and dissect a fish. I bent and altered a five-inch wobbler so it resembled a crippled minnow and caught a seven-inch fish.

I doubt many fly fishermen have given much thought to using flies in the same manner. Dry flies would present a special challenge. I guess you could tie them unbalanced to float awash. Maybe that's why the no-hackle patterns, revived in recent years, work.

It's interesting how fishing experiences seem to support certain theories. I've noticed a perfect wet fly imitation is not always as tempting as one tied with a wing or hackle askew. At other times the perfectly tied fly doesn't seem productive until a few fish have roughed it up. You might claim that's because of the time of day or better water, but it could be, "the rougher the fly, the better the catching."

Have you ever tied on a slightly deformed fly and found it extremely productive? Then you lose it and try a new fly of the same pattern, only to find it less productive? I have.

I know fishermen, much to my horror, who beat up a wet fly before it ever hits the water. They singe the wings, clip the hackle and then fish it with confidence and success.

We always had a box of "marked down" flies that for one reason or another didn't measure up to our standard of quality. These flies were often faded after too much exposure to sunlight in our display window. Or they had oversized or undersized hackle, had a wing missing or tarnished tinsel. Some had been dropped out of the trays and crushed inadvertently. At any rate, they were not perfect flies, so the price was reduced.

Some fishermen would buy these flies for their kids and wives. Then the men would be disgusted if the cheap flies produced the most fish.

We had a customer who frequently pawed through our box of rejected flies, choosing only a few of the most severely damaged. Then he would brag about how he caught a whopper, a quick limit or the only fish of the day on the cheapest fly in the box.

Perhaps we should have been charging more for these "wounded flies"?

There are many perfectionists who would argue that precisely tied flies produce the most fish. I remember one customer, John Hopkins, who would search through my wife's flies until he could find a half dozen perfect Hopkins' Variants. The flies worked so well for him that he was determined only Sig could produce what he wanted. After we retired, he phoned and said his fishing would never be the same. He pleaded with us, so Sig agreed to tie his Variants for one more season. Then we gave him the name of a tier who could meet his expectations.

That Should Be Outlawed!

It was one of those days when the salmon flies were on the water in profusion. The flies were being forced out of the main current in toward the bank where I was fishing. This mass of natural food was accumulating directly in front of me, so I was catching twelve- to fourteen-inch rainbows cast after cast.

Two old-time fishermen above me started to gradually move downstream. They quite obviously were just out of the huge insect flow. Finally, one of the men couldn't stand it any longer. And, coming closer, addressed me: "What the h... are you using?"

I showed him the fly, its construction and size and explained to him why I was scoring on each cast. I then rigged him up: I took off his long-shanked Woolly Worm, tied on one of my Sofa Pillows, and told him to move into the area I had just vacated, which he promptly did.

In a few minutes, he had caught his first fish and then several more.

His partner from up above joined him.

"What did he tell you? What do you have there on your leader?"

The first fisherman patiently explained how I had given him what I called a Sofa Pillow.

By then, I was moving downstream, but not so far away that I couldn't hear the second fisherman exclaim: "They should outlaw a fly like that."

Fish Stories,
Fish Places

Fatso and Fussy

While I was growing up in the 1920s and 1930s, our family's favorite sport was fishing. Limits were large, fishermen few. Surplus fish were never a problem. They could be smoked, salted down in kegs, presented to locals who did not fish, or given to the hospital. No one in our town released a fish intentionally.

In the fall of 1936, I went to West Yellowstone, on the upper Madison, to teach school. There, Don Martinez and his young son, Stuffy, introduced me to the novel notion of releasing fish.

Driving north out of West Yellowstone, past Baker's Hole Campground and beyond the Madison River bridge, I saw Stuffy's bicycle parked on the upstream side of the highway. If you have driven this road, you probably have noticed the willows on both sides of the highway. Before the earthquake of 1959, Hebgen Lake backed up on both sides of the road. The upstream side supported a large population of six- to eight-inch eastern brook trout.

There Stuffy crouched, catching and releasing those scrappy little brookies. While I watched, I noticed a considerably larger fish feeding close to the alluvial sandbank.

"Maybe it would be fun to catch and release that one," I thought.

Later I tried; the fish took, was brought in quickly, and released before I could change my mind. It was a beautiful fish, in spite of a slightly deformed lower jaw. As I watched him scoot away, I dubbed him Fatso because his girth almost equaled his length.

That fall I caught Fatso several times. He was always hungry, feeding from the same mossy cover, not at all choosy as to fly pattern. I considered Fatso my personal friend. When fishing season opened the following spring, I could hardly wait to check on how Fatso had wintered. He hadn't lost any weight and was as gullible as ever.

When school got out, I took a summer job with the Forest Service. They had begun a campground improvement program in Madison Canyon below Hebgen Dam. They wanted to allow campers in established areas, and part of my job was attempting to enforce this policy. The switch from "camp anywhere" to "campgrounds only" met with considerable resistance among perennials who for years had staked out their own campsites in the canyon. The tensions that built from my day's work were relieved by evening fishing.

One of my favorite stretches of the Madison River in the canyon was the area where Beaver Creek entered the river above the Old Beaver Creek Campground. To get to this spot, I crossed Beaver Creek on a log bridge. A large rainbow trout lived in a deep hole above the bridge. Many small fish often fed close to the bridge, but never ventured into the pool above. I could usually catch one of these small trout, but never that larger rainbow, until an old-time summer home resident on the creek suggested I was too impatient.

"Cover 'er with thirty or more good casts with a dry beetle bug, and I think you'll get 'er," was his advice.

Even though his suggestion went counter to my experience and general method of covering water, I followed his advice. The fish finally took on the forty-first cast, and since it was his fish in his backyard, I felt duty bound to release it.

It was the largest fish I had released up to this point. It gave me a squeamish feeling, a sense of loss. However, we thought Fussy was a good name for her; she was a one-fly lady and had to be coaxed. That summer Fussy came to a beetle bug several times, never on anything else, and never on fewer than thirty-five casts.

Those two fish, Fatso and Fussy, were the first in a long line of happy memories of fish caught and released. One of the additional thrills I get out of fishing, besides the simple joy of casting modern equipment accurately enough to get a fish to rise to a fly, is catching a fish I know I have caught before. It is like, well, it is like coming home.

Fatso and Fussy are no longer there, but several other of my friends are: Herman the German and Mr. Big, whom you will hear of later. They were both alive and well, swimming in the Madison River, when I last dropped by for a visit.

How do I know? you might ask.

I know because they are in water designated by the Montana Department of Fish, Wildlife and Parks as "catch and release."

Old Shep's Paws

Uncle George had a dog named Shep who followed the plow as George tilled the virgin soil up in the Horseshoe Hills. When the team would kick up a jackrabbit, Shep would give chase. While the rabbit would race away at top speed, Shep would set a more leisurely pace and would be far behind as the two would disappear over the hill. We wouldn't give Shep another thought as we watched the dark soil turn under the chrome-like blades of the two-bottom plow. Invariably, as we returned to the ranch yard, Shep would appear alongside, mouthing a live and literally run-down rabbit.

Once back in the ranch yard, Shep would hold his head high and display the rabbit to all in a "look what I caught" sort of way. Then he would settle on his haunches with the rabbit between his paws. The rabbit would eventually get its wind back, dry off a bit and inch away as Shep's attention drifted to other things.

The image of Shep with a rabbit between his front paws flashed through my mind the last day I fished Charlie Creek.

Charlie Creek is a spring-fed, open-meadow stream that runs parallel to the Missouri River valley where I grew up. Last fall while looking for a few eating-size trout, I hurried along, hitting only the better spots. I quickly caught three small browns with a dry hopper. Then as I floated the hopper along the edge of a deep run, there was a disturbance near the head of the pool. Water boiled as though something of good size was moving under the surface. It must be a muskrat, I thought, but it might be a fish.

The creek bent sharply at the pool's head. The water was shallow there but was piling up on the right bank, where it deepened. I stood inside the bend, some fifty feet from my target. Without moving, I threw a high, not-too-slack line cast.

It wasn't my best effort. The fly landed nearly three feet short of its mark, but it floated lightly as it settled on the water. A large wake moved downstream toward the fly and the fish slurped it in. I had to strip hard, step back and lift the rod.

"Hello, Mr. Big!" I said as he responded to the hook by racing downstream through the deep water and into the shallows. There he turned, like a sleek athlete swimming laps in a pool, and headed back.

I fought desperately to keep the line free from the grass at my feet. The fish repeated his first performance; down again he shot to the end of the pool, and back. Even against the pressure from the sharp arc of the rod, he was running deeper. On the third run I thought he might race all the way to the Missouri River. However, he finally turned down into the mossy bottom; there he lay in about two feet of water.

With a landing net I could have scooped him up easily. I waded out to pick him up by hand. When I was within arm's length, my front foot sank into the soft mud bottom. The motion to drag myself out of the mud triggered the fish to action. As he darted off, my tippet broke, the leader flipped into the air and rattled down the line guides.

"How does any fisherman, experienced or not, justify the loss of such a fish?" you ask.

Well, you don't expect to land them all.

I calmed down as I tied on a new fly, all the while rethinking the action of the last few hectic moments. First, I had been lucky to have seen the fish at all, and luckier yet to have taken him on such a sloppy cast. After the strike, everything had happened as it should, my reaction to the runs, the way I played the fish, everything except the way I stumbled on the stream bottom. I consoled myself realizing it would be easier to catch him the next time around.

I worked away from the spot, casting into a few more riffles until I caught one more small fish for dinner. Then I felt ready to give the pool a calm and critical look, and to plan the next attack.

As I explored the approaches to his pool, I made several casts to positions where I might find him feeding in the future. I noted leader and fly action at the drop spots. When I left the stream, I felt that I knew the water. Catching him was just a matter of time.

A week later I returned to a spot where I could study the field of battle while assembling my weapons. The surface of the water was calm and undisturbed. Mr. Big was there; the question was, where? I watched for another ten minutes without seeing any tattletale signs. Then I chose to move cautiously to the spot where I had taken him before. This time my position was better as I made a soft cast to shallow water a foot off the far bank, well above his feeding position.

"Oh, no!"

This day he had chosen very shallow water close to the weed bed and deep water. The instant the butt of the leader touched the water, Mr. Big shot off, home free.

I clipped my fly off the leader and went home, too. I had learned one more thing about him. His time was running out.

The third week when I stopped to check on Mr. Big, there was only one fish working at the tail of the pool. It turned out to be a two-pound female brown that I caught and released. The following weekend I was back again. A few small fish were rising, but my fish wasn't there. Still I worked the head of the pool carefully, but with no results. I spent the remainder of the afternoon just watching. My rewards were the earthy alkaline smell of soil and dry grass and a beautiful view of the snow-fringed Rockies as the sun set.

I went home with the feeling that maybe my mind had exaggerated the size of the fish and I would spend next Sunday afternoon elsewhere. However, when the weekend rolled around, the thought of the big fish in such small water lured me back to the pool. The season would soon close, and this might be my last try for him this year.

I arrived earlier than before, and stayed well away from the bank as I approached the stream. There were no signs of fish feeding, but a hatch was developing. Moving upstream, I scanned the stream's bottom for light gravel spots that might be evidence of spawning beds. I saw a few, but none was the size that would indicate Mr. Big had helped in their making.

Moving below the big pool, I heard a noisy splash. There was my fish, or one just as large, slurping flies along a deep fast pocket less than two feet wide and just off the bank where I was standing. As I watched, I was amazed by his attacks on the insects, his explosive force as he slapped the water taking the mayflies as they funneled to him from the riffle above.

Mentally, during the last few weeks, I had cast to every possible spot where this fish might be feeding. I had avoided every pitfall. Now, the solution seemed too simple: Stay with the same fly pattern, use a 4X tippet, and cast out a short line over this small pocket of water, since the current was swinging insects to my side of the stream.

I flipped the fly easily to the head of the drop-off where the water darkened. The fly moved only inches before the fish struck. The sound and suddenness of the strike caused me to rear back on the fly rod; the fly pricked the big brown's jaw. He came flying out of the depth and actually landed on the flat and grassy bank near my feet. Instantly, I jumped between the fish and the water. With my knees on the bank facing the fish, I realized my haste was wasted, the fish wasn't going anywhere. He was on his belly with pectoral fins extended, body thrashing. I marveled at the helplessness of this fighting creature, out of its element on the grass bank.

Without touching the fish, I grasped the fly between thumb and forefinger, backing it out of his jaw.

We had each won a round. It took but a moment to secure the fly in my hat band.

Still watching in awe, I lifted the fish in a scooping motion with both hands and arms extended, with no real thought except possibly to guess his weight.

It had been fun. Why end it here?

I dropped him back into the darkness of the pool. I thought if he weighs six pounds now, what will he weigh next season?

My arms were still extended as he slipped back. Or were those Shep's paws I was seeing?

Shep, you were a pretty smart old dog. The pleasure is in the pursuit, whether it's jackrabbits or big browns.

Forest fires of 1988 changed the scenery in some of Pat's favorite haunts along the Madison River in Yellowstone National Park.

A Narrow Escape
An Introduction to Firehole

Bears were more plentiful in Yellowstone Park back in the 1930s, and there were a lot more fish, too. One day I was alone in the shop, the fly orders were piling up, customers were bragging about slaughtering fish on the Madison, and I hadn't felt the tug of a fish on my fly rod since the last stagecoach left town. I thought I could almost hear fish splashing water in Baker's Hole.

Something happened I won't attempt to explain. I suddenly found myself standing at the old Iron Pipe Hole, my favorite on the Madison and just ten miles from West Yellowstone, with my fly rod in hand. Why I was holding the rod is a little easier to understand. I always keep my rod on the car rack, set up, in case of an emergency like this.

I had hooked my fifth fish and had it on when, on the opposite bank, out of the woods, came a big, beady-eyed black bear. To make matters worse, that rainbow jumped across the river from me and almost under his nose.

The bear took a look at my fish, a quick look at me, sniffed the air, put one foot in the river and headed in my direction. This confirmed my suspicions. He didn't like me taking that fish. He could have sniffed the fish on the line, the ones in my creel, or just ME! That last thought was slightly unnerving. I had heard of people climbing trees, even with snowshoes on, in an emergency like this, but I never gave it much credibility. Anyway, I hadn't climbed a tree in years.

Ashamed of the way I had to treat the poor fish, I did what I thought was best. Before the bear could get that second paw in the water, I hauled the fish in and threw it to the far bank.

Well, that was an educated bear. He had been thrown plenty of things by tourists in cars. In two bounds, old bruno made it over to that tasty morsel. He was back to the bank, mouth watering, before I could make my next cast.

What could I do but give him the four other fish? But that wasn't enough; he wanted more. I had been pressured before and since to catch fish for myself and friends. Never was I pressured more than by this customer, Mr. Bear. After what seemed like hours, I finally satisfied his taste for trout and he let me go back to my fly-tying table.

Iron Pipe Hole to Madison Junction

The iron pipe of the Iron Pipe Hole on the Madison River is no longer there. It was removed when the new road was built in the 1970s, but the water drainage, crossing the road underground from left to right, is still visible. Your best clue for locating it is the river turns away to the right as you pass it about ten miles east of West Yellowstone.

It's best to park just beyond the hole at the elk meadow and walk down river.

The water upstream from the tallus slope to the Iron Pipe moves fast and shallow, attracting few fishermen. From the Iron Pipe upstream to Madison Junction, the water runs deep year round. It is difficult to cross, and can be fished from the highway side.

However, those who ford the Firehole at the Junction and fish down through the meadow with wet flies and back with dry flies usually have nice catches. When the season opens in the spring, this water carries a tremendous quantity of insect life in all stages of development.

Remember, because of the warmer temperature of the water, the food cycle is advanced considerably. Nymphs are popular in this water, as are dries. Stay with sizes that float well, in the 12 and 14 range.

Grayling

I had been teaching in West Yellowstone. When Ranger McKnight asked if I would like to take a trip into the back country, I jumped at the chance. Although I enjoyed my teaching, the opportunity to spend a couple of days outdoors was always a pleasant change.

Mr. White, the district supervisor from Bozeman, was in town. He had six milk cans filled with trout and grayling fries, which were to be planted in the high country. Instead of the usual metal covers used on milk cans, cheese cloth was put over the top and tied in place. This allowed for a better supply of oxygen and the ranger felt it would be adequate to keep the minnows from escaping.

Packhorses were loaded with the cans. Ranger White planned only one stop en route, a ranger cabin on Wolf Creek where the cold spring water would keep the fries active. Hebgen Lake, the headwaters of the Yellowstone and Grayling Creek, had been the sources of the minnows.

All went well as we headed out: three rangers, me and six cans tied onto three horses. At the overnight stop we lifted the cans from the saddle packs and laid them in a backwater hole in the cold water of Wolf Creek. The extra oxygen and the moving cold water made the grayling minnows more active than we had intended. The next morning the cheesecloth was off their two cans; the grayling had an early taste of freedom. We hoped the escapees would survive, and just for a little fun we renamed Wolf Creek. It was now Grayling Creek, even though the map makers never recognized our change.

We continued our trip, depositing the rainbows and eastern brooks at the designated backcountry lakes.

Time went by. I opened a tackle shop in West Yellowstone. Occasionally, I wondered about the grayling that had escaped, but I hadn't

Hebgen Lake.

had the time or occasion to investigate until one summer when my sister and her husband from Pennsylvania came to visit. We went for a boat ride on the Madison, and I told her my grayling story.

"Did you ever catch a grayling in Grayling Creek?" she asked.

"Never did," I answered.

"Have you tried? I'm curious to know whether the 'milk-can, self-planted' fry survived and have left offspring."

To please my sister we stopped where Grayling Creek enters the Madison. This may sound like one of Ripley's *Believe It Or Not* stories, but I did catch a grayling. And that became my favorite spot to stop when guided customers or friends wanted me to "produce a grayling."

The grayling has always been one of my favorite fish.

I remember, as a boy, one of our car trips to Hebgen Lake. While our family now lived "down river" at Three Forks, we often drove our old vehicle up to Hebgen to check on the place where my grandfather had lived.

On this particular trip, my mother parked on a bridge at the mouth of Grayling Creek and sent me down to catch fish. It was just a matter of minutes before I returned with a grayling dinner for all of us. Grayling were plentiful in Hebgen Lake, the Madison River and the Big

Hole. In the Park, grayling could be found in the Madison, Firehole, Cougar Creek and Duck Creek. Grayling lived in the cold, clear waters of the Gibbon, Taylor Fork, West Fork, Cliff Lake, Ice Lake, Elk Lake, and of course, Grayling Creek.

Elk Lake is right in the middle of grayling country. If you leave Henry's Lake and drive up over the hill, you'll find Elk Lake and big grayling. You'll find smaller ones in Red Rock Creek.

In the 1940s and 1950s only dirt roads led to this area. Few fishermen knew of the spot where Darrel Parker and I fished one July day in 1973.

We would have been smart if we would have left the dogs home. Gunner was Darrel's dog, and he was trained to dive for and retrieve big grayling. Ashley, my red setter, didn't distinguish between big grayling and smaller ones. Any fish was fair game to him. He loved to stand on the bank and watch me play a fish until it was flopping near shore. Then he would charge into the water and nudge the fish the final few feet.

It wasn't long before Gunner had taught Ashley the pleasures of the deep-water retrieve. I hooked a big grayling and Ashley perked his ears. He dove into the water and disappeared. I thought he'd never come up. But when he did, he dropped the fish at my feet, looking at me with an expression of pride. He was happy as a clam. I was saddened by the fact that he had learned that trick from Gunner.

Big grayling are disappearing from our waters. Are there too many Gunners and Ashleys? Or are there too many fishermen who keep too many big fish?

It Fishes Well

or The Odd Fish

If you are reading stories this winter about places to go fly fishing and can't wait until spring, think about New Zealand. I highly recommend it for a number of reasons.

Besides the fishing, you probably have heard about the wonderful scenery, the renowned homespun English hospitality, and the favorable rate of exchange. If you are a lamb chop lover, add that to the growing list. You can buy a freshly butchered hogget (nine-month-old lamb) for the price my wife pays at the local market for a few frozen chops. Then too, they do speak a language similar to ours. Of course, as in any other place south of the equator where you might go, they speak faster than you are first able to follow. This is especially true of the telephone operators. I mention these lovely lassies because they are one of the first links in the chain between you and great fishing.

I'm always surprised by how many fishermen come back from New Zealand happy with everything but the fishing. Articles they have read seem to overemphasize the size and number of the fish and how easily they can be caught. So the fishermen failed to do their homework. Besides contacting someone here at home who has fished in New Zealand, the traveler should write to several sources in New Zealand who will give you general information.

In a nutshell, but with exceptions: The North Island is best for lake and lure (streamer) fishing; the South Island is known for stream and dry fly fishing; fishermen on both islands use nymphs. Decide in advance whether you want to try back-country fishing. If you plan to hire guides you must book early; fishing on your own has its own rewards. There are few no-trespassing signs to rivers—the government owns the boundary lines—but traditionally you contact landowners before going on or through their property.

Ask any Kiwi what the fishing is like in any of his rivers and you will be thrilled. You can expect him to answer your question in one of two ways. One, "It fishes well." Maybe I had better capitalize that statement. "IT FISHES WELL." Now you are enthusiastic. His second possible response is, "The river contains an odd fish."

Let's dwell first on the statement: "It fishes well." He probably has never even fished the river, or he hasn't since his youth. He does mean it has fish in it. He is encouraging you and recommending this river to you. Yes, It fishes well. Not easy, not hard. You will expect to see fish. It might be in flood stage, there may or may not be a hatch. It might be slightly discolored, but it is easy to get to and he'll give you directions. You need not bother to ask what flies you should use. You wouldn't remember the names anyway. He has been helpful and you are pleased.

Now, what about that odd fish? It doesn't mean what your dictionary says, "not paired with another."

The word just sizes up the Kiwi's expectations.

"You'll not find a lot, but there's an odd fish there once in a while."

Favorite Stream

I am frequently asked: What is your favorite stream?
The answer I give is not an attempt to evade the question, as accused by one of my friends. It is in fact an answer that comes directly to the point.
"There were 10 pretty girls in the Village School.
There were 10 pretty girls in the Village School.
They were short, fat and tall,
But you can't love them all
And you can't marry ten pretty girls."
With fishing streams, the variety in Montana (and elsewhere) is expansive. They all produce a world of pleasure!

One Fishing Day of Many

If you were to outline the elements of a perfect fishing experience, they would surely include: 1. Knowing how the weather and water conditions would affect the fishing at the chosen place; 2. Understanding the equipment and method to heighten the experience; 3. Having the skill necessary to get results; and 4. Sharing the experience with the right person. All of these ingredients were present one day on my last trip to New Zealand.

To fish with Bob Speden, a salt-of-the-earth New Zealander, home town Te Anau, South Island, is to add the necessary seasoning to make a day fishing a memorable experience.

I first met Bob on one of my earlier trips to New Zealand. We had similar backgrounds. At that time, each of us owned and operated a tackle shop; he in New Zealand, I in Montana. We each guided fishing customers. Bob's wife Sarah took care of their shop when he was on the river, my wife Sigrid did the same for me.

Now back in New Zealand, I had been fishing in the town of Gore with some friends from the United States. After they went home, Bob invited me to come to Te Anau for a few days of fishing. We had each sold our shops, so he was not pressured at this late date in the season by customers. It became a case of two guides doing what they liked to do best—fish.

Deciding where to go this day was the big question—one that I was happy to lay at Bob's feet. The discussion started during a leisurely breakfast: Canadian bacon, fried eggs, toast with marmalade, and tea. While we ate, Sarah fixed a lunch and packed it in the "chilly bin," the New Zealand term for ice chest.

Bob looked out the kitchen window, studied the cloud cover over Lake Te Anau, checked breezes that rippled the lake's surface (for wind direction and velocity), and listened carefully to the radio about the area's weather forecast. He phoned two locals before the last drop of tea was gone. Then we packed our gear in the Land Rover and were on our way.

The fishing possibilities near Te Anau are endless. I thought of the Eglinton, the closer Whitestone, or Waiau, maybe the Mararoa or the Oreti. We could drive to those places. Bob asked me again if I wanted to choose the spot. I didn't. He was still undecided when we left town, but I did know it would not be the Eglington or the Waiau since Bob headed north on Highway 94 toward Mossburn. As we approached the settlement, he again noted weather and wind direction.

"We are in luck, Pat. Unless conditions change, we should find things right on the tributaries of the Aparima. We will take a look at the water under the upper bridge that crosses the 'Hamilton Burn'."

New Zealand names have two sources, the Maori names that we Americans have some trouble pronouncing, and the names given places by the early settlers from the British Isles, mostly from Scotland. In Scotland, a burn is what we call a small stream, creek, or brook and New Zealanders are happy with the Scottish word.

My experience in this area was limited. I had dropped in on a few spots on the upper reaches with little success. Bob had been raised in the area, had walked the tracks well before the New Zealand government had started buying up small stations, clearing large sections of native brush, building roads, fencing, and spreading superphosphates. Bob had once commented that he wanted to revisit places where double-figure fish were known to have lived before the government wrecked the natural environment and we Americans caught all the big fish.

Before we got to the bridge, on an impulse Bob turned off the macadam onto a gravel road that led up a narrow glen. We soon stopped, set up our rods, and got into our waders. We stepped carefully over the low sheep fence into a cultivated field and walked a short distance toward an opening in the line of scrub. There before us was a beautiful pool of the Braxton Burn. Even though we stopped short of the stream, two submarines with periscopes showing raced out of the shallows and into the deep water, which was lined with overhanging bushes on the left bank.

"I guess we blew that," was my comment to Bob.

"It's good to know they're still here," was Bob's only reply. "We can try for them later if you wish. There still may be undisturbed fish at the head of the pool."

"Bob, I don't see how a stream this small can support even two fish that size, let alone several more."

"There is more food here than you think. They rest in deep pools like this one, but they do a lot of cruising both up and down stream in search of food. Fish move here when the lower river channels out."

We waded carefully across the shallow riffle well below the pool. At Bob's suggestion, I tried without success a small Adams at the pool's head.

Bob had crossed to the right bank with me, moved upstream, and located a lesser brown feeding.

"Want to try for this fish?" he asked.

"How big?"

"Maybe two or two-and-a-half."

"Pounds or kilos?"

"Pounds, Pat."

"You can have him," I said.

The night before we had tied a few flies. Bob had needed to replace a few English patterns he liked, one in particular, a #16 mole. I tied several for him. He took the fish, a three-and-a-half-pounder, on one of those flies.

We would have spent more time on this stream, but we saw another fisherman moving downstream toward us, so we went back to the car and continued to the bridge across the Hamilton Burn.

Most bridges in New Zealand are built high enough to be well above any flood waters, and this bridge was no exception. There was a parking spot down from the road near water level on the downstream side of the bridge. We parked there and walked back up to the bridge to get a good view of the stream both up and down. My first thought was that this stream carried considerably more water than the Braxton. Upstream from the bridge, vegetation crowded the water line on both sides for fifty yards where the river came in from the right, the heavy current on the left.

Looking down, the stream flowed away as it doubled in width and ran shallow at about ankle depth to the riffle below. What appeared to be fourteen- to sixteen-inch fish were feeding on mayflies riding this smooth surface. I had hoped for something larger.

Bob was especially interested in the upstream side across from the car.

"Do you want to see some nice fish, Pat?"

Why bridges and big fish often go together I will never know. I peeked over the upper edge. In a small pocket away from the main current and close to the shadow of the bridge lay a near double-figure brown. There was hardly a break in the quiet surface as he took the mayflies that drifted down to him. Now I was starting to get excited.

"You have two choices to try for him, go upstream and drift your fly down, or work up from under the bridge."

Both options presented major problems. Above the bridge there was little room for a back cast, too much chance for exposure because of the high bank. The approach from below and under the bridge left little overhead casting room and unwadeable water next to the bridge support. In each case the advantage was with the fish.

It was easy to see why this fish hadn't been caught. My attempt from below caused him to drift out of his feeding position into deeper water.

While I was trying for this fish, Bob spotted one below the bridge that was considerably larger than the rest, and farther downstream. The fish was feeding close to the bank nearer where the car was parked. Bob insisted I try for him.

Having learned the need for a safe, careful approach, I waded across the stream well down in the area where the smooth water broke into the long run below. Once on the far side, I moved up almost directly across from the spot where the brown continued to feed. I made several upstream casts to measure out the necessary line, hoping to judge as accurately as possible the distance needed to float my fly to the fish.

Something about the way the fly drifted disturbed me. I checked the leader and fly carefully, changed to a new 5X tippet and on Bob's suggestion added a fresh fly, a mole.

My first cast to the fish landed some ten feet above his position, inches from the far bank. The fly followed on the slack line the feed stream of insects being delivered to the fish by the current.

The fly slowly drifted that ten feet. Closer and closer to the waiting trout. Finally, with hardly a visible movement, a bulge appeared on the surface; the fly disappeared.

It's debatable where you get the most pleasure: in the presentation of the fly, the strike, the fighting, or in landing the fish. Probably to most dry fly fishermen, it is the strike, or in this case, the action better described as the take-that point when you first feel some pressure on the tip of the rod.

The fish headed upstream into deep water. The reel sang in the key of B, not an unpleasant sound. Slowly the line was worked back. Each time his runs, though strong, came back a bit easier. Finally the fish was guided into shallow water, where I backed the hook out and released him.

Bob also caught a nice fish near the bridge. The two together, if we had kept them, would have weighed close to 10 pounds.

Bob's choices continued to pay off, and our skills were sufficient to land every fish we hooked. We came off the stream with one fish well over six pounds, which we kept. Several others as large were carefully released.

It's great days and friends like these that keep fishermen on the river.

Where, When We Fish

I have told you how we fish. Now, briefly, let's look at where and when we fish.

In June, we fish close to West Yellowstone, both wet and dry (depending on water conditions). We start with the Madison in the Park and the Firehole. We also hit the South Fork of the Madison, Cliff, Wade, Hidden and Smith lakes. Then we try to fish the Big Hole the second and third weeks of June. If you get there earlier the water is usually pretty high and you have to fish with streamers.

In early July, the Madison is our main dish. Side dishes include Fall River, the Firehole, Ruby and the upper end of the Yellowstone, if it clears. The water in the Centennial Valley is dessert. We try to follow the salmon fly hatch; if we're lucky, we hit it on three or four rivers—Madison, Jefferson, Gallatin, Big Hole—for thirty to thirty-five days. It's always nice to mix in a few days on the Smith before the Missouri gets good.

In August, we go back to the smaller streams, the high lakes, the Gallatin, Bechler, Boundary Creek, small meadow streams, the Yellowstone in the Park.

September and October find the Madison and Firehole in the Park good again. We also try to hit the Bechler and the Yellowstone.

As you can see, five months is hardly enough time to sample the area's premier fishing spots.

Fishing Goes Collegiate

From a 1947 Missoula newspaper

Yes, you can learn many things in college. Look at Penn State—there they teach you how to fish!

And that's not all—you get credit for "Principles and Techniques of Angling" at Penn State, according to an article by James W. Strupp in the September-October issue of "The Outdoorsman." Students flock to learn fly tying, fly casting and other techniques from the veteran angler, George Harvey. Other universities have offered fishing courses informally, in fact, Doc Schreiber once taught such a course at MSU [Montana State University, now University of Montana, Missoula—Ed.]. But Penn State is believed to be the first institution to give the course for credit. Several west coast colleges have expressed interest in the Penn State program.

Well, how about fishing classes here? MSU is a natural for such sport, as it is for riflery and skiing. With students furnishing their own equipment, cost of the course would be negligible. And instructors shouldn't be hard to find. For example, Pat Barnes, graduate student in education, has won state fly-casting contests, winning the Bozeman and Livingston contests in 1941.

If this thing developed into intercollegiate competition, MSU anglers should be able to cast a line with the best of them. How about it?

Fishing
Extracurricular

On Painless Hook Removal

With the ever-increasing numbers of people fishing, more young people, more women, more retirees, more people are getting hooked.

It could happen to you.

The first question you should ask is how do you keep yourself from being hooked.

Take a look at a professional guide and you'll note he wears glasses, a hat that protects face and neck, a jacket and shirt to protect head and arms. Guides are also careful in crowded areas and are conscious of the danger at all times.

Despite the precautions, guides do get hooked, just like everyone. So what's the best way to remove a hook?

About thirty-five years ago, Dr. John H. Steel, chief surgeon at the Veterans Administration Hospital in San Francisco, came to West Yellowstone to fish. That summer John inadvertently buried a fly in my lower lip. It didn't ruin our fishing that day. We clipped the leader and left the fly embedded; we'd take care of it later. That night, after some deliberation, he pushed the hook through, increasing the size of the wound, clipped off the point and barb and then removed the hook. The method he used is the same one described in the American Standard Red Cross Manual. It's probably the same method your doctor would use in a similar situation. My lip was sore for some time.

The following summer, Dr. Steel returned and was excited about another method of removing a hook from a fisherman's flesh. He had read a technical description by Theo. Cooke, M.B.B.S., of South Australia. On one occasion earlier that summer he had used the new technique. He praised it highly, saying anyone could do it.

The next summer he sent me a page from the *New England Journal of*

Medicine. The *Journal* story described the process, with diagrams. Up to that point, I hadn't had the courage nor the incentive to try the new system, but I filed the *Journal* story for future reference.

Then, during the summer of 1966, Dr. M. Merrill from Phoenix and I arrived back in West Yellowstone after a day of fishing to find a group of fishermen waiting for the doctor. One fisherman had snagged his friend in the back of the neck with a long-shank #4 Grey Ghost Streamer.

"Would the doctor remove it?" they asked.

We looked at the fly, which stuck out from his red and swollen neck like a bumble bee. The fly had been well mangled during earlier twisting and turning attempts to remove it. The patient was feeling no pain as he and his friends had visited a few of the nearby bars while waiting.

I dug out the *Journal* article, which Dr. Merrill read. He seemed impressed and I thought he was ready to try the procedure.

But he took me aside and assigned me the job of removing the hook. We would need his black bag to make it look official, he said.

The patient, the perpetrator of the act, and a group of sympathizers followed us to the Westward Ho Motel. We seated the patient in the best possible light.

The doctor and I stood behind him, examining the wound. I felt a nervousness like that experienced by a young surgeon ready to perform his first operation.

I had procured the heaviest piece of leader material available (20-pound test). Dr. Merrill and I huddled over the patient like two mother hens over a wounded chick. Following the instructions (see diagram on page 153), I looped the leader around the bend of the hook, depressed the shank into the skin (very important), and gave a strong jerk. The Grey Ghost flew fluttering overhead. Doc and I looked at each other as we heard the sound of the hook hitting the wall.

"Please Doc, will you quit fooling around and get the fly out?" pleaded the patient.

In his best bed-side manner, Dr. Merrill asked the man to place his finger on the fly. He tried.

"Who! What! Where did it go?" he asked.

Dr. Merrill was busy looking for blood, found none, and dabbed the spot with something from his bag.

"I did nothing," he confessed. "Pat got it out using the new Cooke method." The minor crisis over, the patient and friends had another reason to celebrate.

Word about the painless hook removal spread fast in West Yellowstone. We removed a lot of hooks that summer. I was always surprised by how easily and painlessly they popped out. Some people treated the incident with little concern, others thought the removal was a major operation.

I posted the instructions on our bulletin board so everyone would have the information.

As a professional guide and outfitter I continued to insist customers wear glasses and protective clothing when fishing. I still had to remove plenty of flies. My only reward for removing a hook came from a young movie actress who, while honeymooning in New Zealand, had been hooked by her husband. I got a kiss.

In summary:

1. Wear glasses, a hat and protective clothing.

2. If you get hooked, study the hook removal graphic and then proceed carefully. Don't be afraid. In the 30 or more years I have used the technique I have never had a failure nor had a patient say it hurt.

3. Get a tetanus shot. If you decide to see a doctor to have the hook removed, ask him if he knows of the method. If he doesn't, tell him about it.

4. Always see a doctor first. Don't try this tactic if you're hooked in sensitive parts of your body, especially around the eyes.

The procedure:

1. Loop a strong line around the curve of the hook and wind line onto the operator's right index finger.

2. Press down on the hook's shank to disengage the barb and position the hook at the angle of entry.

3. A sudden strong pull on the loop, parallel to the shank, frees the hook painlessly.

4. Treat the puncture wound.

5. Get a tetanus shot if needed.

6. The hardest part of the procedure is deciding to proceed.

Removal of Fish Hooks

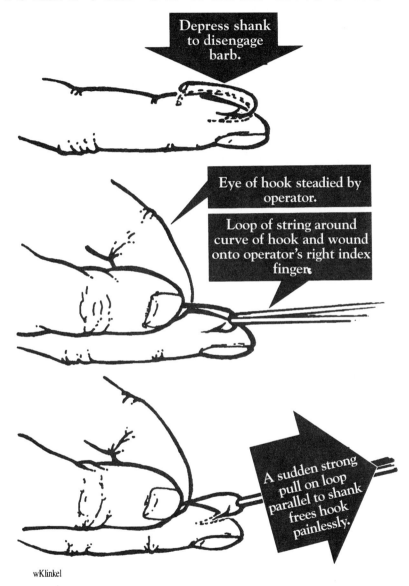

Depress shank to disengage barb.

Eye of hook steadied by operator.

Loop of string around curve of hook and wound onto operator's right index finger.

A sudden strong pull on loop parallel to shank frees hook painlessly.

wKlinkel

153

Warden, Poacher and Me

Dating back to the early days on the open range when every man was the law, there has been an uneasy intolerance toward higher authority. This has certainly been true where fish and game are concerned.

During my youth, the Montana Fish and Game Department consisted of a small cadre of wardens. Those few employed were often local men who had the same background and philosophy as the residents of their district. Those wardens ruled their areas with a free hand, more or less, dispensing justice within guidelines only loosely prescribed by headquarters. Those days, of course, are long gone, but they produced many vivid stories about wardens who were outsmarted by poachers, or vice versa, in games of one-upmanship. Only occasionally did outsiders become involved on the winning or losing side. But in the story that follows, you might say the warden and the poacher maneuvered to a draw, and an outsider was the winner.

The year was 1922. Someone was shooting beaver on the lower stretches of the rivers forming the Missouri near Trident. There was little evidence; no shots had been heard, and there were no tracks into or out of the river areas where dead and skinned beaver had been found by ranchers, fishermen and other friends of local warden "Frank M." No strange cars or even local ones had been seen.

The warden, whose job included the responsibility of keeping beaver alive for legitimate trappers, was worried. One dead beaver along one of the rivers wasn't much to be concerned about, but reports indicated there was a serious problem in all three drainages. The warden decided the poacher had to be trapped, even if it required his full-time dedication.

It was obvious to Frank from the start the culprit was floating the river at night. He was somehow locating the game for an easy shot, skinning the animals on the spot, and then floating on. The warden knew the country well, since he was born in Montana. He realized the closest place to launch a boat on the Jefferson River was at Willow Creek. On the Madison, the road came close to the river at a spot known locally as Black Point. On the Gallatin, one of the bridges crossing the river out of Belgrade toward Menard seemed a likely spot. Dead beaver had been found below all of these points, but none above.

Once A Poacher...

John, an older cousin of mine, lived through the Prohibition days in Montana, while selling a little moonshine and working occasionally at other questionable jobs. All the relatives disapproved of John's way of life, and they were sure he would come to no good. But John fooled everyone. He moved to the West Coast, married a lovely young woman and they raised a fine family.

However, John couldn't escape all his old ways. He didn't adhere to the fishing laws when he lived here, figuring a fish was his for the cooking. And he always remained a poacher. When he'd come back to Montana, he'd hunt and fish without conscience, and without a license. During one trip back, I asked him pointedly whether he had a license. He seemed insulted that I should ask, and he assured me he had bought one from my wife, Sig, at the fly shop. Knowing John as I did, I checked the records. No license. The next day he bragged to me that he got along just fine without one.

Later John visited Montana during pheasant season.

Perhaps to needle me a little, he asked, "Pat, is the limit this year three pheasants or five?"

"John," I said, "You're out of touch. The daily bird limit has never been printed on a license. Anyway, you certainly wouldn't find it on the only license that I know you ever bought—your marriage license."

Frank reasoned the take-out point could have been Logan or Three Forks, but more likely was farther downstream—probably Trident or even Lombard. Lombard at that time was a flag stop on both the Milwaukee Road and the Northern Pacific, a stop that had two railroads through it but no wagon road.

Inquiries among residents at these locations uncovered evidence that a so-called salesman with heavy sample cases often boarded trains for Butte. Frank knew this was the first real break in the case, but more leg work would be required. A week at Lombard, presumably to fish Sixteen Mile Creek, was the next order of business, with enjoyable evenings spent entertaining the station master's daughter.

Regrettably for Frank, that came to an end as the salesman never appeared. Trident was the next stop. With his recognizable Model T coupe parked out of sight, Frank wandered along the Missouri River headwaters, fishing rod in hand, looking for evidence of a possible take-out spot for a boat—a place not too far from the depot. He gave special attention to a "hobo jungle" camp used by men of the road. It was deserted most of the time, with only an occasional occupant. There were a few empty cans, two old campfire pits circled by rocks, one orange

Headwaters of Missouri River
Three Forks, Montana

Early postcard.

crate, and several cottonwood logs that had been dragged into place to form crude frameworks for shelter. Frank passed the spot several times before he noticed an old rusty corrugated piece of roofing off to the side of the camp and near the river. It lay partly concealed by wild rose bushes and it appeared it hadn't been disturbed for years. However, he was curious, and closer inspection revealed it had been lifted recently.

Frank pushed a toe of his fishing boot under one end of the roofing and flipped it over. There, neatly folded and wrapped, was a canvas boat with oars, a long object in an oilskin, and a rain slicker, which, when unwrapped, disclosed a cooking kit. The stick-like object wrapped in oilskin turned out to be a Winchester .25-20 rifle with a home-made silencer screwed to the end of its barrel. A flashlight had been neatly assembled on top of the barrel with batteries positioned in the bored-out stock. It was an ideal gun for night shooting, which was highly illegal even then.

The warden quickly ran through a list of possibilities. Where was the poacher now? Was he watching from a distance? Would he come back for his equipment, and if so, how soon? Had the poacher's supply of beaver run out, making the operation fruitless. Should Frank set up a stakeout?

Considering the time he had spent in the vicinity, Frank doubted his presence in Trident had gone unnoticed. He had been neglecting his other duties as well, so he decided to end it there. He burned the boat and oars, removed the flashlight from the gun, and had a gunsmith work over the threads on the end of the gun barrel.

Needless to say, the poacher, without his tools, either gave up poaching, thankful he hadn't been caught, or moved on to greener and fresher pastures with new equipment. In any event, the beaver killing ended in Frank's territory. Years later, when Frank died, a young warden and I found the rusty silencer in the bottom of a trunk in the old warden's cabin.

Why do I consider the episode to have ended in a draw? The warden must have considered himself a winner. Why else did he keep that silencer, except as tangible trophy of his one-upmanship? And the poacher? Although we know nothing of him, I can still imagine him bragging to his friends: "I made a killing on beaver, right under the nose of one of the best wardens in the state."

I said earlier the only winner was an outsider—in this case, me. Warden Frank M.—Uncle Frank to me—gave me the poacher's rifle, the same gun I used to kill my first elk when I was 15 years old.

More warden stories

Snake River: The gang had a good morning on the South Fork. My fishermen were all talking and eating their lunch when a canoe pulled up.

"How's fishing?" the warden asked.

The younger man in our group began bragging about his catch.

"May I see them?" the warden asked.

"You'll have a hard time doing that," another in our group replied.

"Is that so?"

"It is, we released all of our catch."

The warden pushed the canoe away from shore.

"I know," he said. "I've been watching you all morning."

Madison River: Two rods, one fisherman in a boat.

"Pull in, Bob," the warden says. "You know, only one rod!"

"Yeah, that's my dog's rod."

Warden sees a car parked along the river. Father and son are cleaning their day's catch.

The warden leaves his car and walks down to the river.

"Nice mess you have there, son."

Son, pointing to river's bank: "Take a look at those big ones under the bush."

Old gentleman is catching fish right and left behind a large Madison River boulder.

The Warden has no waders, so he calls out to the fisherman: "Will you come in and show me your fish?"

Old fisherman: "It took me 30 minutes to get our here, I'm not going to move for anyone! I've got waders, have you?"

Two men are fishing. The warden approaches. One of the two takes off at top speed. He crosses the river and stops.

The warden catches up.

"May I see your license?"

The fisherman finds his license.

"It's fine, why are you running?"

"The other guy doesn't have one."

Game Warden Marshall was driving the road between Manhattan and Belgrade. He noticed a young boy fishing Baker Creek.

He walked over: "Do you have a license, young man? No? I guess I'll have to arrest you."

"You will have to catch me first."

The boy darted away.

The warden walked back to his car, drove it over to a home not too far away and knocked on the door.

The boy answered the door: "Well, I guess you caught me."

"Is your dad home?"

"Yeah, I guess so."

The three sat down and talked about the importance of having a license.

The boy got by with a warning from both the dad and the warden.

A Streamside Meal

Enjoy the natural taste of a streamside Montana trout lunch. First, clean a freshly caught trout. Place it, along with a strip of preheated bacon, several slices of tomatoes and onions, on aluminum foil. Season to taste.

Then roll it up tightly in the foil and toss it onto a bed of red-hot campfire coals.

Cook from three to five minutes, depending on the size of the fish. Remove from coals and let it cool for a minute. The skin will slide right off and you're left with a great lunch to be enjoyed in a natural amphitheater only Montana can provide.

Wading Tips

It's an unwritten law with beginners that if they put on a pair of waders they should immediately get their feet wet. Don't do it. Remember, often fish are feeding within a foot or two of the bank. Catch these first; then wade if the width of the river makes it necessary or if you see feeding fish on the other side. Most of the wading I did when I was young was to retrieve and save a fly from a tree or bush on the other side of the river. I had few flies and they were precious. I'd wade upstream, cross and then swim back to the bush. Of course as a youngster you don't worry much about waders.

Here are some tips for wading:

• Carry and learn to handle a staff.

• Don't wade if you can't swim; know your limits.

• Don't cross your legs; shuffle your feet and keep them close to the bottom as you feel your way along.

• Turn sideways to fast current.

• Plot your course well ahead; take advantage of slow water.

• Buy waders that fit; use felt bottoms or something better than rubber.

• Have a short vest for wading deeper holes and keep your landing net on your back out of the water.

• Stay out of water that's too deep and too fast.

• Learn from past experiences. For instance, the water behind a big rock is always deep, but it will gradually become shallower. Also, you can wade to the upstream side of a rock and fish both sides and downstream.

• Scrub your waders and shoes when you leave a stream. Mud can protect bugs and parasites, which can be carried to the next stream you fish.

• If you happen to fall, try to float downstream feet first with your knees bent, and try to float toward the side of the stream where your car is parked.

Catch and Release

Most of us who fished Montana streams and rivers during the first half of the century have reacted favorably to the "catch and release" movement.

I have to admit, I had mixed emotions the first time I released a nice two-pound rainbow. I watched him move slowly through the shallows of the Madison and then flash away.

The trout revives, the angler reflects.

Was this "catch and release" more enjoyable than "catch and keep"? I think so. Possibly another fisherman will catch and keep my released fish, but I'm sure he'll never be skillful enough to take them all.

"Catch and release" has enhanced the sport for me. My rewards have been: I've learned more about the streams, more about when fish feed and where they are feeding. I find trout in locations others have disregarded.

I think back to my hometown when fishermen were few and rivers were teeming with fish. The fish caught were eaten; the main reason for fishing was to "catch and keep."

Only a few locals fished solely for recreational value; their fun was in catching large fish or their limits.

As tackle was refined and the limits became more restrictive, the sport grew in popularity. Phrases like "limit your catch" and "catch and release" became the slogans of the new fishermen and of many organizations that promote sport fishing.

It's a movement you should become a part of, because it will help keep Montana a special place for fishing for future generations.

Safety on the River

1. Water: Watch water levels, especially on Montana's rivers below dams, where water can rise quickly. Watch currents behind islands and rocks, they can turn your boat quickly and throw you off balance and even capsize your boat.

2. Boat: Practice safety. Stay down and don't overload one end. Wear life jackets and don't move around. Don't put too many people into the boat.

3. Winds: Get to shore and protection in high winds. Be on the lookout for snags or blow-downs.

4. Low bridges: Bridges can be too low to float under, especially in high water. Also, Montana ranchers have been known to string barbed wire across smaller streams to keep their cattle home.

5. Look ahead: Don't be careless in the boat. Look ahead, keep your oars in the oarlocks so you don't lose them.

6. Lightning: If a thunderstorm moves through, get off the river quickly. You can turn your boat over and get under it for protection, unless it's metal.

7. Logjams and channels: Stay away from logjams, they create dangerous currents. Side channels can be an adventure— sometimes too much of an adventure. They might even lead you to a hayfield.

8. Lifejacket: Wear the right size and keep it buckled.

Gearing Up

The Well-Equipped Fisherman

We all have our favorite fly fishing equipment.

My mother's was simple: a cane pole ten to twelve feet long with a line tied from butt to tip every two or three feet that extended from the tip about the length of the pole. She added a two-foot leader and a good grasshopper hook. She didn't carry much else—a stringer for her fish and extra hooks or line went into her coat pocket.

Times have changed. Today, fishing jackets are as popular as all the equipment they carry; the many pockets offer a great temptation. (Just think of all the things you can pack along!)

If you stopped along the Missouri River near Craig and asked a fly fisherman to empty his pockets, you might find: several boxes of flies, a leader assortment with all tippet sizes, an extra reel or spool, fly floatant and line cleaner, some lead, a hook sharpener, leader clip, head net and insect repellent, a knife, insect collecting material, rain jacket, fish scales, measuring devices, hook sharpener, and a few favorite extras. In the larger pockets you could spy a pocket camera, a streamside lunch and maybe a soda or beer.

Of course, a few necessary items would be dangling from the jacket: scissors, hemostats, a hook sharpener and sunglasses. Hanging over the back of our fisherman you could find a landing net; a creel would be draped over his shoulder. Then, there's the wading staff.

Far be it from me to suggest that you don't need all that gear, which probably adds ten pounds to your frame. But I do like the idea practiced by some duck and pheasant hunters who know the limit and take just enough shells to bag it. I said I like the idea. I don't exactly follow it.

Where we fish and how we fish determine our needs, so they vary

enormously. Some of the better guides I know carry a complete kit in a convenient bag. It holds all the possible materials their customers might need. The average fisherman doesn't need as much.

My equipment is well organized, so I know right where to find things when I need them. Here's what you might find me carrying if you see me along the Missouri:

• Two things hang from a leash on my fishing vest: A leader clip and a small knife. The knife is more than a knife, it's of the Swiss Army variety with a file, scissors, a hook degorger, a screw driver and a blade.

• I don't carry a net unless I'm in a boat, because I release fish in the water, beaching only the large ones to make that task easier.

• In the back of my fishing vest is a rain jacket, and sometimes a sandwich or candy bar. In a front jacket pocket, I carry one fly box holding flies I plan to use that day (It's a pocket that I can open and close with one hand). Another pocket will hold a few leaders and two or three coils of tippet material.

When dry fly fishing I also carry a floatant in my vest, even though most of my flies are sprayed with silicon before I leave home.

• In recent years I have found a wading staff helps me get to where I want to go, faster and safer.

• A safety pin hooked under the brim of my hat comes in handy occasionally. Speaking of hats, a good fishing hat takes some time to find. It should blend with the background, protect the head, face and neck from the sun and sharp hooks, and it should stay on in strong winds and provide some protection from rain. Many fishermen neglect this important piece of equipment. If you find a good fishing-hat maker, don't keep it a secret.

That's about all a fisherman needs, except a few personal items. Other things, whether hanging from your vest or cluttering up pockets, will probably just get in the way.

In my fifty years of fishing, I wonder how much time I would have saved and how many more fish I might have caught had I not spent quite so much time fishing for my knife in a cluttered vest, untangling my line from a dangling net, changing flies unnecessarily or chasing a blowing hat downstream.

The Right Equipment

If you have a friend who's a fly fisherman or if you know a friendly tackle dealer, that's where you should go to discuss your tackle purchases.

You'll want equipment that fits your needs, depending on the rivers and streams you'll be fishing.

Catalogues of reputable tackle dealers are another good source of information. In 1921, when I was twelve years old, I purchased a one-dollar reel, an enameled line and a three-piece Shakespeare bamboo rod from the May Company in Chicago. I knew they would work for me until I could afford better equipment. The rod, with several necessary repairs, lasted through fourteen seasons and beyond. The reel and line were replaced long before.

As modern life needs have been refined, so have those of fishing tackle. My first rod was made simply and quickly so it could be sold inexpensively. Other bamboo rods I have purchased through the years have been made by craftsmen, who, by and large, have begun to fade from the scene. That's because fiberglass came along and became a material of choice for inexpensive fly rods. Now, graphite has replaced fiberglass as the most popular rod material.

Bamboo, fiberglass and graphite have different characteristics and your fishing friend or tackle dealer can help you make the best selection. Most likely, it will be graphite, and your rod will cost anywhere from $25 or $30 to several hundred or more. Fiberglass rods will generally be among the cheaper rods.

If you decide on bamboo, be ready to pay handsomely, for few craftsmen are making quality bamboo rods these days.

A good reel can be as important as a good rod. Reels, too, have undergone change. The first reels were just spools to store line when it wasn't in use. A handle was eventually added to make it easier to retrieve line. Later additions included adjustable drags and "clickers" to let fishermen know when the line was coming in or going out.

Reel shapes have been changed through the years to speed line recovery and to hold backing and running line. Today's reels range from the simple to the complex, but generally they're lighter and smoother to operate than earlier versions.

DOUG O'LOONEY PHOTO

Pat, in 1948, was the first to use a McKenzie River boat in Montana.

Pat's Definitions

Bait. A highly exhilarating beverage of the fisherman. Guaranteed to remove varnish. Will counteract snakebite, heat, cold or bad luck.

Bait-casting reel. A contraption, invented by Satan, designed to come apart, get out of order, or snarl up on all critical occasions.

Bait-casting rod. A sporty name for a fish pole costing more than ten dollars.

Catch and release. The perfect answer to the conservationist's fish prayer. The biggest fish are generally released about midstream.

Creel. A fragile, wicker basket in which to hide a worm can, carry a fly book, slicker, fisherman's almanac, etc. Occasionally used to hold small trout.

Fish. A fighting denizen of the deep that lures millions away from home and business. Fish usually grow a lot faster after they are taken from the water.

Fisherman. One who rises early in the morning, disturbeth the whole household, goes forth with high hopes, returneth home at night smelling of strong drink, and the truth is not in him.

Fishing. A disease for which there is no cure; catching but not contagious. It formerly affected only savages, small boys, and village men, but it now attacks presidents, judges, doctors, lawyers, ministers, priests, and 15 million others. In extreme cases the fever can be reduced by placing the patient in the hot sun or in a heavy thundershower.

Fishing camp. A place to wear out old clothes, eat half-cooked food, fight insects, and act red-blooded. Someone always spoils the party by going fishing.

Fishing liar. A fishing term used by every angler to describe all other anglers. A piscatorial prevaricator.

Fishing line. An expensive piece of string used on a reel. Guaranteed to snarl, snag and break at the right time, thereby creating the necessary alibi for the whopper that got away.

Fly fishing. Wading in cold water, sitting down in it now and then, hooking a fly in the neighboring brush, and calling it sport.

Fly rod. A rod that is sold by weight. The lighter the rod, the heavier the price.

Fish hooked. A fish hooked in a part other than the mouth.

Guide. A true conservationist in disguise. Takes you where they were biting good "last week" when the water was or will be lower, higher, clearer, wetter.

Worm. Greatly scorned in public, by sportswriters and walleye fishermen, but secretly used by most of them.

Index

At home on the river.

Rod and line respond under experienced hands and eyes.

To Dave Shors,

Without you this book of my fishing memories would never have been written.

Thank you for your never-diminishing enthusiasm, for your expertise, for your suggestions, and for the pleasant hours we spent discussing and working on how to best compile and put my notes into print.

Pat Barnes

GEORGE LANE PHOTO

Dave Shors is the associate editor of the *Independent Record* in Helena. He has spent countless hours fishing the Missouri and other Montana rivers and streams during the past twenty-six years.